Alabama Light & Power Co

The Chalice of Bedlam

a novel by

Lynn Strongin

Plain View Press
P.O. 42255
Austin, TX 78704

plainviewpress.net
pk@plainviewpress.net
512-441-2452

Copyright © 2011 Lynn Strongin. All rights reserved under International and Pan-American Copyright Conventions. No part of this book may be reproduced or distributed in any form or by any means, or stored in a data base or retrieval system, without written permission from the author. All rights, including electronic, are reserved by the author and publisher.

ISBN: 978-1-935514-82-4
Library of Congress Control Number: 2011929485

Cover art: Earthdaze by Mark Heine
Cover design by Pam Knight

Acknowledgements

An earlier version of "The Crack in the World Through Which Light Shines" first appeared in *Word For Word*, an online journal edited by Jonathan Minton.

An earlier version of "Morning Glory Blue Jeans" first appeared in *New works Review, 2008*. "Magnolia's Second Hand Rose" appeared in slightly different form in *Magnolia: A Florida Journal of Literary and Fine Arts*.

Thanks to Pam Knight who, when Susan Bright unexpectedly stepped through the door of death, carried on with grace and courage.

For Melody Poirier & Swannee's memory

and

For Susan Bright, the light of whose life went out before Alabama Light & Power Co went to press, but whose light encouraged me thru some of the darkest years of my life.

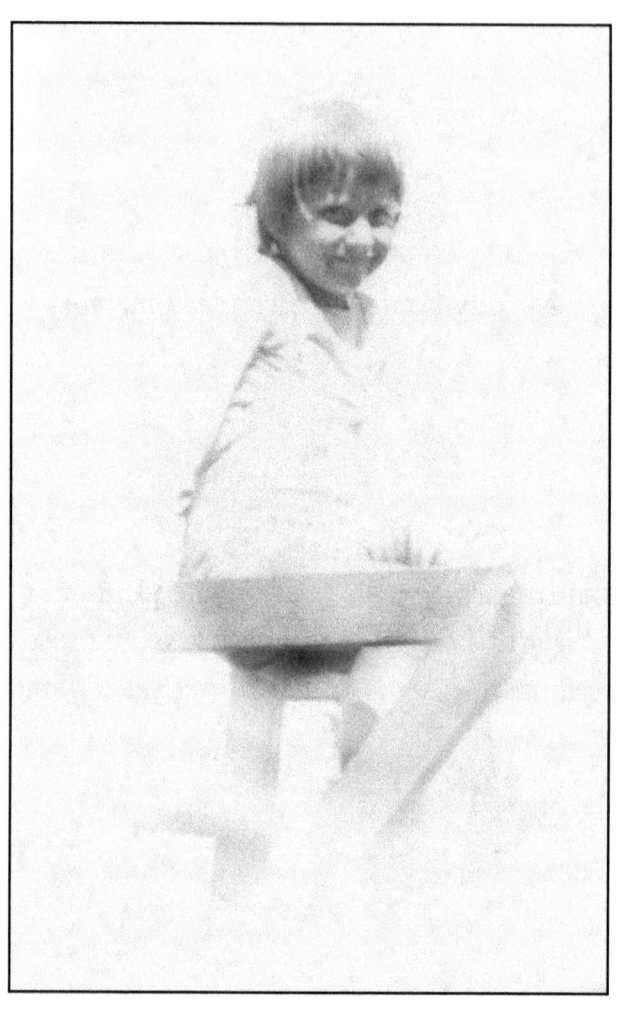

Lynn Strongin, 5 years old, Jungle Gym at Golden Beach, Miami, Florida, 1944.

Contents

Transparent Circus   9

     The Crack in the World Through Which Light Shines   11
     Morning Glory Jeans   25
     Magnolia's Second-Hand Rose   31

Hawk's Eye View of a Buxom English Teacher   41

     The Drive Down Coast: Sarne and Lee   43
     Jo-Jo   61
     Child Revealed   79

Plenteous Redemption: A Trilogy of Stories   83

     Not Rain—Liquid Sunshine: Plenteous Redemption   85
     Brown Rabbits: The Meek Shall Inherit the Earth   95
     Johnny Jump-Ups: Those Who No Longer Dream   97

High Kicks   101

     The Coldest Wrists   103
     Amelia's Dreams   109
     The Sweater: Treading the Rim of Medicine   115
     Bringing Bright Honor Home   119
     Sobranies   125
     Bitterroot   131
     Twilight, Heart-Side   139
     The Horse Would Tell It Differently   147

Burning: An American Dream—A Story in Four Sections 155

Blue Air: The Cutting Edge 157
Boys Who Die Virgin 159
Initiation: Rite, Sanctuary 163
Closure: The Boy 167

Alabama, Long Gone 169

Setting Out the Costume 171
Fanfare 175
Trembling 179

Books by Lynn Strongin 183
About the Author 184
About the Artist 185

When I was traveling with the circus in the 70s I loved the South. So different than my background growing up in Alberta's Rocky Mountains and northern prairies. It felt like a different planet, not just another country. Even the insects looked and sounded different (remembering my one and only—and painful—encounter with fire ants and bright scarlet colored wasps in Mississippi.) I remember some of the show folks we traveled the country with had their origins in the South and were extremely uncomfortable in the Pacific Northwest – even though it was still part of their own country – it felt foreign and strange to them. Until I had traveled the southern US, I had never heard a Canadian accent. After a year in Dixie, I finally traveled north again and crossed the border in southern Saskatchewan and for the first time I heard the accent everyone had been teasing me about. But to this day I still tend to develop a bit of southern drawl whenever I drink bourbon.

Melody Poirier

Lynn Strongin, 9 years old, New Rochelle, New York, 1948.

Transparent Circus

These are fascinating days: I am nine. The curtains shabby are old but once rich velvet: this is setting the scene for my entire life. A camera on the side catches us. We are transparent, that close to breaking.

For Cassandra who understands the sadness
         & for CR especially on the passage of Moll Flanders

Lynn Strongin

Doll, photograph by Deborah Munro.

The Crack in the World Through Which Light Shines

The loading dock held crates of shrimp. It was where we kids hung—literally, our feet perched on a lower rail, our hands grasping the top wooden rail and our heads hung over the water. Most children spoke with a drawl. Eternity Gasworks and Harmony Brick Factory stood out on the low horizon.

You saw the generators lit up at night with tiny dots of illumination. We called them the fairy lights. The same kind of lights blew and burned in a southern storm over the concrete plant across the river. You could hear the ubiquitous thrum of motors. The night air was heavy as a lady of the night redolent with honeysuckle and lilac. Wood dust too, scented the air. The people who moved were largely circus people, down for the winter to the South—in the surreal filmic air of the South they appeared to be enacting a transparent circus.

Watching the hauling in and the iridescent light kept us stoked and amazed. We never roved far from this feeling. We saw it as the amazing light and it lofted us. Buckets of ice stood nearby. Like those granite quarries I had left behind in New England where the ledges filled with snow and ice. These wooden slat boards glistened with beads of salt water. Fish traps had a bayonet glimmer they flashed back like grapeshot.

This world of Bonneville belonged to my doll, Alabama. She was one hundred years old and had thus survived the Civil War. Maybe she belonged to some little girl in the North who rocked her back and forth while her daddy was gone fighting the South. Maybe she belonged to some leggy little girl in the South who rocked back on her heels, hugging her doll while her daddy fought the North.

Alabama was what I named my bisque doll when I was nine. She broke apart like skywriting rumpled up, wrinkled by winds. She was the bisque doll who shattered so early in my life it was as though she opened the curtain on the drama of my life itself. She took center stage. I lost a century in losing her.

Mother rarely drank bourbon. When she did, I saw the crack in the world through which light shines. I saw her hold the chalice of madness, of Bedlam. This is about her and the world we lived in as kids.

"You were born to be torn in half," Mama shouted as I ran to catch Alabama. "It behooves you to behave yourself," my mother raised her voice.

We had a fight and the doll went whirling through the air and struck the wooden bedpost which was shaped like a ball of bread dough. One half her head was blown off like heads of children I'd seen in newsreels in the war.

It was during some difference of opinion, some dragon fight between Mama and me that Alabama shattered. I covered my mouth with my hands not to cry out loud. When I picked her up her beautiful and elegant miniature face was broken in two: one half held one eye, one the other. When I took her to the bathroom with what I called the crystal window, I shut the door to be private. I knelt on the toilet with the lid down so I could hold Alabama up in the shrewdest light possible. Thus, tried to piece the two halves together like a puzzle of burnt clay, she assumed an odd expression.

I had learned to bite the dust and twisted my toes in it while mother was grieving the dead-long-ago-doll. "All she survived, and now she's gone."

I mimicked one of mama's favorite phrases at junctures of crisis, "We've come to a fork in the road," and turned on my barefoot heel and left the room.

When I came forth, I said to Mama, "I spoze something marvelous is going to happen."

"Humph," she said. "It isn't the first time you're supposing that.

A greenback was on the telephone table. I looked down at the grave, bearded face of Abraham Lincoln telling me things were going to work out right. But they never were okay again. Not between the South and the North. Nor between mother and me. And not on your life for Alabama, who right in that very moment I married to Abraham. Abe with honesty, the green running thru his face on the five-dollar bill. It was 1947.

My next determination was to see how I could mend Alabama, if ever. I went for the glue pot.

This surgical procedure of my trying to glue together the two halves of a cracked visage was but the first preview of that film I was to observe a million times. Her tragedy was the crack in the globe through which light shone. It was a stairwell, light and dusty, illuming splintered gold wooden rulers. One walked the numerals, breath drawn in as if to blow a balloon. Ringing up a curtain on a drama, at times opaque, at times translucent. In her hands was the chalice. She was one hundred years old and we called the thimble she held — made of waterless, crazed porcelain — the chalice of Bedlam. Why? Because when Mama felt she was going crazy in the Alabama light, she'd say she was going to Bedlam.

"What's that?" I asked.

"A place. A hospital in England for the insane."

"An asylum?" I asked.

She nodded.

Then I asked, "What's that?" pointing to the thimble with rosebuds which the bisque doll held.

"That's the chalice of Bedlam."

"A sparrow couldn't drink from it," I said.

"We must send her to doll hospital," Mama said.

I choked and gulped. I shook my head fiercely 'til blind-sighted with tears, at last I nodded.

We sent Alabama to the doll hospital; she came home with a different face. Her visage was cracked and crazed with tiny fracture veins. She looked both horrified and horrific like a doll who had been in a house that was bombed. It was like when I lost my legs to polio at age twelve. I went into the hospital with legs and came out without them; frozen legs unable to move. The doll with her bashed biscuit-colored head has lit up my life.

○

Mysticism, illness and the South were interlocked. I was torn between Mother and Father, the North and the South. It was then that I realized in the South strife continues, bandages were still being tied (in the forties) in the Civil War of the heart. A Red Cross nurse leans into the dust but it is too late. It was then that I realized we are all players in the transparent, translucent circus of life. The one who is the clown cries through smiles, smiles through tears. Clowns always made me mourn. I was detached cruelly and very young from the traditional ideas of the family. Hence, ironically, it made me safe. Divorce split the nuclear family of two parents, two children into an odd number—three.

We rested in a shoebox of a rented room in Florida where we had gone for the divorce. We had to establish residence outside New York where the only grounds for divorce was adultery proven with photographs. To establish residence you had to live one full school year in the state. That meant September through June. Our silhouettes were visible at a certain hour between the wolf and the dog at sunrise and sundown. The Celtic twilight of the fairies shrouded us as though we were enacting a pre-figuration of the coffin.

Mama pulled up the window shade. We looked down on a dusty little street below. "Look at it as if it's a motion picture," she said to me.

And ever since, even the night I contracted polio, there was a crack in the globe thru which light shone. I have looked at this life as though it were on the silver screen.

I think of mother as the enchanted princess who bore her child in her sleep, the past dusted with a film of pearl. In early childhood I became a planner of dreams in which nurses bound up civil war fatalities. A moment too late, they were on the battlefield. They had no option.

The bird who nearly garroted himself in my wheelchair, gave himself no karate chop but flew his brother to the doll who broke.

Polio left me in a ward of children who became the new measure of my existence. An old military installation turned into a rehabilitation tank for stricken children. Victims of contagious diseases were lodged there; overflow spina bifida and the freak cases— like hydrocephalus, the girl whose head was too large to be contained in anything but a cart in which she lay for a bed. And one special child with a clandestine passion, a child Amelia Earhart, on whom I secretly fastened my gaze. All were soldiers, victims of a battlefield strewn so thickly one could hardly see the ground. Like my one-hundred-year-old porcelain doll that shattered in the spring of my childhood, they all held the invisible chalice to their lips, the chalice of Bedlam.

○

The South was a cradle of deaths. Eucharist and evidence. We were in the deep South. My best friend, Sipsie asked, "How can angels pull on nightgowns over their wings?"

It is a rich land but the southernisms differed from northernisms. Expressions fascinated, puzzled and riled me by turns.

Eulalie-Sue said, "I'm tickled pink to get an 'A' in 'rithmatic."

I knew just what she meant.

But when she said, "My daddy, he'd give his right nut to get published in the *Atlanta Times*," that was another pair of sleeves.

She drew out each syllable saying it, "Atta-Lann", dropping the "t", which my mother said was a slovenly way "t'speak".

I first screwed up my face as I always did at too much sun. I then nodded as if I knew. There was very little I then knew about the South. I learned.

Alabama Light & Power Co

I did know we were residing, because I could not think we'd live there for long. I had given Alabama her name because we were living outside Birmingham for the time being. If this was the Bible Belt, we were at its buckle.

"We're the buckle of the belt," was a thing Mama told me one night.

I recalled after Eulalie-Sue said that about her daddy, in the white-pink southern dust, she all at once crossed herself and whispered, "In the name of the Father, Son and Holy Ghost."

"Why is the Ghost holy? Why did you cross yourself now?" I asked.

"Dunno," she shrugged. She ran off, turned round and thumbed her nose, grinning, repeated, "Holy, Holy, Holy."

Maybe it meant something like tart, which I knew was a lady of the night. When I got home, I told Mother about Eulalie-Sue saying her daddy, the writer, would give his right nut to appear in the *Times*.

"Pardon me?" Mother asked.

"His right nut," I repeated putting together then that he had a left one.

She said, "That's not an expression used by eight-year-olds."

"Well," I said, "Eulalie-Sue and I are born the same year, 1939 and only one month apart. Now if the fact that she was born in January and I was in February makes her that much older, allow me grace."

"Grace?"

"Let's pretend I'm one month older."

"Well, you're not," Mother retorted. Then she did what I hated, drew me by the chin up close to her eyes and said, "I think there's something a bit strange about you."

Always the indicting word was "strange," not mean, not foolish or stupid, but strange. It made me feel orphaned, an Ishmael, a changeling.

"It's not an expression that concerns girls your age."

"But I'm my age and I'm concerned...Eulalie-Sue said she heard her mother say it."

I dig my fingers into my skull 'til I bleed. This is what I do when I am frustrated. Like so may of our conversations, this one turns to sky writing. First I can see it, then I cannot read the letters any more for they are blown away by time.

I wondered if this expression is related to the batch of white balloons I found in daddy's highboy while my parents were still married. I puzzled over why adults would keep a box of balloons, then figured it was for my sister's birthday or mine. But why all white. "Put those away," Mother had said when I started to blow one up. "It won't blow up. It doesn't concern children."

One day I put my underpants on backwards. It wrecked my day.

Mother said, "I could see it if you were a boy." She threw up her hands in a stage gesture. She had wanted to be an actress but didn't have a strong enough voice.

I sighed. It was always that or another kind of indictment of my behavior.

"I knew a girl who..." and this girl, of whom she knew many varieties, had done precisely my wrong behavior and suffered the consequences.

"I knew a girl who sassed her mother and she..."

I didn't want to hear about any more benighted girls but I did put together that this behavior, pulling out the forbidden white balloons, and talking about Eulalie-Sue's daddy's right nut went together somehow. They were interlocking pieces of a puzzle.

○

The earth was pink and the sky white. It was August, 1945. We were walking the thin line between depression and elation, between rebellion and acceptance. We were kids of nine and ten. Americans were dropping the bomb on Hiroshima at the other side of the world and then on Nagasaki.

In the South, the visible and invisible came together for a brief moment. Flickered light was shining upon Gas Works, the Printorium and the Euphoria Brick Layers Union #29. Then the earth was plunged into a deeper blackness than it had ever known. Once in a blue moon, invisible and visible came together, balanced for a precarious moment and made sense of the world. Married. We may have exemplified, without our knowing it, the last battle of the *woh'* of *no'thern* aggression. The Baptist preacher shouted about something called the Kingdom of Heaven that was like a mustard seed because it grew, became greater than all herbs and this mustard seed shot forth branches. Because he was a preacher (whose name I don't remember) the tree was the Tree of Heaven.

We didn't see that. We saw the rear side of the circus more *mizzable* than a month of rainy Sundays. There was no protection, as St. Mark promised, for the fowl of the air to rest under its shadow.

I went to school up north where I learned about Ichabod Crane the skinny tall schoolmaster who was created by Washington Irving. Now I attended school down south where every other body was an Ichabod Crane.

I went to school down south where the hygiene teacher said to nine-year-olds, "You're still knee-high to a grasshopper, but girls, when you start applying cosmetics, remember to wash your puffs."

We weren't anywhere near that time. We learned from Isabella that our nude bodies, if we were girls, and we all were at that time—our body in its birthday suit featured two nipples and a puff. Fanny was a girl's name but not mentioned as the part of your body you sat on.

Women drank bourbon, speaking with a drawl. There were scarlet colored wasps that stung in Mississippi—a state whose name we remembered by hoping twice on each foot through the word until we got to the "IPPI" and giggled as little girls and no other species on earth do.

All changed. It was a global change. The very earth we stood on was now pink rather than earth-brown.

Yes, the earth was pink as a Spalding ball you bounced and lifted your leg over and the sky was white as candles or Monday's wash on the line. The South was cradle deaths, Eucharist and evidence. Catholic girls were forbidden to play with themselves so sex was put on a back burner.

I could see the devil had a red tail and you went to hell if you didn't put your slippers under your bed.

○

The South is a red pepper grinder alongside a battered cookie tin that had been raided by three generations — both on a kitchen sill, paint blistered, window panes with cataracts. One looked for the sky to crack and yolk to run. We needed one another desperately, yet we reached out with fear and trembling. One could die of blood that ran from a prick at the spindle. One hungered for something beyond doorknob biscuits done in gravy. We were girls without insurance, still young, we ate fried chicken and drank gravy. We were both underground voices and an illuminated colony.

We tried one last time to fix the doll's face; one eye was moved up higher than the other, though, and her mouth had lost its sweet expression.

"What do you think?" Mama said. We had circled the day she went into and came out of the doll hospital in Birmingham.

"Not much," I said. "She has the wrong expression."

"What's wrong with it?"

"She looks mean. She looks as if she has it in for someone. She doesn't have the sweet expression she had before."

"Maybe she got fed up with looking sweet."

"She wouldn't." I was haunted by the grotesque; I pressed her bisque brokenness to my washboard flat chest.

That cold chalice. It was with me when I made music for the children in the asylum. It was with me that horrific two-hour slot in time when I was dragged into and out of the asylum. Like the cold, an adventure in the world's frozen place, a migration that alerted the blood in my heart, the rhythms of its muscle.

In a way this is an Alabama ghost story. I liked bad weather, crews working feverishly to clear snow paths. The southern picture-window weather was without interest to me. I was a drifter, a lover, an outsider.

The whole South was invalid, convalescent, a translucent ghost borne on a gurney. It was photographs behind windows, the milk of memory drunk by a thin cast. When girls got on the rag, some rolled up their sanitary napkins under rugs. Joni did and when moving day came her mother rolled back the rug to her horror to find twenty stinking pads, the blood still visible. If you told someone you'd seen a ghost, they would simply nod unblinkingly.

This was the land of King Biscuit sky. The land where women sat on back porches, even the great southern actress who said, "I like taking tea with my chickens. They don't talk back. I'm a bit of a theatre bird."

Everyone was a bit of a theatre bird. The painful feeling that nothing happens in the South was relieved by the brilliance of peacocks, those southern swanked up chickens.

Our mother treated us quite adult. When our father called, she'd hang up and light up. "Your father had that bedroom tone in his eyes." She had more reasons, I figured, to be frustrated with him than you could shake a stick at.

I was with our daddy while he took our mother to dances at the asylum. This was for diversion. "We've gradually become so diverted," she'd say to me while she was ironing, burning triangular cigarette colored skeletons into whatever white thing she was ironing, "so diverted that by now I probably am a disturbed person."

Troubled, I thought keeping calm. We're a performing family. We thirst for curtain call. Keeping cool in the clutch is one thing we admire to the hilt.

"You give me the buzz, you must be my honey," I said to the tall long legged girl in plate-glass who looked back at me, fastening her green eyes upon mine. It was the deep South. Here Eucharist was broken, epiphany occur but right beside the Alabama Light & Power Company. It stood near the river with its reddish dust. It was poor. Ironically this great power stood there. Generators. They were generational passed on from the Mason grandfathers to the fathers to the sons. It was a male world.

Except for the sweetness. That was from the women. We had the moxie and sipped on our cokes, got high on our first aspirin and coke while they ate their fries and grew obese on pulled pork.

Vanilla Log was the second hand store near the dock. Grandma Faye had unearthed treasure from her attic to fill this store, which stood in a wood fish shack. It held children's pillows with stripes and with animals, odd egg cups but not her ancient-looking doll Miss Hickory. Miss Hickory had a face made of hickory nut, with roses painted on her cheeks. She was a one-hundred-year-old doll, hands clenched in fists before her as if she wanted to be picked up and hugged but instead had to put steel into her backbone to harness all the power and light in her kingdom. A boy doll, Sampson, stood nearby as if he kept guard over Miss Hickory. Sampson's arm broke off at the elbow. The children called him Stump.

Grandma Faye's became an ice cream parlor in summer where old and young alike came, stirring up clouds of dust in their tin lizzies, eating all flavors of ice cream. The kids liked blue ice cream best of all, which wasn't blueberry but was bubble gum. Sundays people came after church, the little girls in their Mary Janes polished like mirrors, their frills dragged in the dust by now. The grandmothers came smelling of elderberry wine in all their finery. Much of it looked like borrowed finery.

The wallpaper flowers and sugar bowls were there but the figures in the paintings got a wiggle on, began moving. They threw electric shadows and magnetic zeroes. I was filled with amazement. Lofted, stoked by the miracle I said to my mother, "I am so filled with exultation."

More often I was mortified. Peacocks dragged about in the dust, those swanked up chickens.

A silky knot of ash blond drawn into a chignon at the back of my neck. A glossy purple clot of blackberry ripened in August sun. They baked in

August. I wanted everybody's story. Class storyteller, I was too shy to become town narrator. But even then I knew that the name of the story was *now*. It was a very large story, because now never remains. As soon as you say the word it become then. As you watch fields of cotton balls flash by from the Southern Pacific caboose they become in the past, become gone.

Quicker'n you can say Jack Robinson. But just as Bob's your uncle, sure as the lord made little green apples, the fruit over ripens and rot set in. The child wants some sugar with her bedtime kiss but looks up with apprehension.

We kids lived in dirt plots of whitish-rose earth. Adults sat fanning themselves behind a flimsy screen door, which rattled like grandpa's teeth in a glass at night. They rattled like Petunia the pig scuttling their hooves like castanets. Sunday school where girls were taught legs are like best friends, always together. Sunday school was over. We'd listened politely to the Hammond-B but wanted privately music that got you up out of the pews and dancing. A little emerald-eyed lizard scooted across the church parking lot. I caught him with the corner of my eye. I was called in from the yard by nightfall but it took me a basset moment to respond. Basset hounds are proverbially slow, slow as molasses in January.

All my rivers flowed on paper: I elaborated so that by age nine, put a bar code on paper and I could make a lyric out of it.

I did anagrams. Seventeenth century astronomers transposed findings into Latin anagrams, rearranged letters of a word or phrase to produce a new word or phrase using all of the original letters. Anagrams exit in our language as links. *Silent* becomes *listen;* *Astronomer* becomes *Moon Starer, Narcissism* becomes *Man's Crisis*.

Down the road from the doc was Jackson Hole where we weren't allowed to go in the dark. At sunset I'd see the butcher's wife exchange her rubber apron spattered with blood the color of holy ruby for her baking apron. Confectioner's sugar and jam and rolled clumps of dough clung to that apron.

We girls know about our bodies. We referred to our pocket books, which like our diaries we must keep to ourselves. Our vaginas were these pocket books, purses; parachutes hat opened at the right touch our orgasms floating down. I mulled this over as I sat playing cat's cradle on the candlewick bedspread or watched Mother make cherry pies rolling out the dough with a scarred old wooden rolling pin, then putting a lattice of pastry in slim strips over the cherries.

Alabama Light & Power Co

The docks were the terminus of town. A mile off freight trains making their southern run from Georgia all the way down into Florida punctuate the night with lonesome whistles which pierced the soul and the ear as a fall can puncture a spinal cord resulting in paralysis. Like a Dutch door, the bottom half stayed closed and the upper part swung open upon a southern night after a day of unbeatable dust that clogged the lungs. In day, one wanted only shelter. By night one longed for touch. Nubile girls with rounding pear breasts, who wore training bras and had perfect cupid bow mouths, and peaches and cream complexions lured me with the tone in their musical voices up and down the scale. I was young, still green and wet behind the ears but I was learning how fiction works.

"Yours 'til I'm asking for your autograph at some stage door," a girl whose name has long since sunk into oblivion wrote in my nine-year-old's autograph book.

One observer of the South who worked a while in the circus wrote me, "It felt like a different planet, not just another country. Even the insects looked and sounded different (remembering my one and only—and painful—encounter with fire ants and bright scarlet colored wasps in Mississippi). I remember some of the show folks we traveled the country with, had their origins in the South and were extremely uncomfortable in the Pacific Northwest—even though it was still part of their own country—it felt foreign and strange to them. After a year in Dixie, I finally traveled north. To this day I still tend to develop a bit of southern drawl whenever I drink bourbon."

○

In the incendiary deep South, the little ice age of hatred had returned. Alabama's state bird is the wild turkey, her nickname The Heart of Dixie or Yellowhammer State. I had a passion for putting out fires: for cooling down the wrath and sorrow, the repression and rage in our divorced family struck by polio. I loved to watch billowing fire smolder in a small ashes. The state motto is an extinct whale and state nut a pecan. It is a rich land but the home of poor people. It is freshly opened ground but hardly new ground which I return to in my seventies.

I say to that state epitomizing the state of mind which is the new South, you give me a lot of buzz but you're still my honey. Something heroic like the hillbillies of the Ozarks, a forecast of heroines coming in the South in the women occurred in my time. Something exotic we ate, pork and pickled vegetable soup, sweet potatoes growing on the honey suckle line occurred to, flash-flooded me with vision, ignited my visions like a firestorm.

Like Eniwetok, drawings of Iceland, Baffin Islands, Canada, and the polar North ignited my imagination. Here was the desperate Canadian tundra. Here were a people composed in a forlorn situation. From northern Scandinavia, across taiga of Siberia to ice bound East Greenland, humans have proven themselves capable of enduring. Earth never thaws.

In the sinkhole that is the South, which sure could stand some cheering, in a prison of heat and racism, poetry flourished and transcended the bars of that prison. The garb of Icelander is fur, the garb of the southern stripped pale down into pastel clothing. But this is the powerhouse heavy into cut. The iron claw in the velvet glove.

The northerners had first pointed to the ships asking what great creatures those were. But they were an animal of another ilk. They came from where there was nothing but ice.

The little ice age returned of the deep South, insupportable wrath. This land never cooled down. There are tortures where people are frozen then broken apart with a manner. These are war crimes, war games. There is torture where people melt with the heat of ignorance and who are ignited by a taper dipped in accelerant. The first I saw in books of the Vikings, the second in day-by-day life, albeit during heightened occasions such as war, illness divorce. The second I saw in the corrugated roofs and water melon juice of the deep South.

Whether where Brer Rabbit exists, or where the ptarmigan sings to the long-tailed duck, the aim of writing is to tell a good story. Homer knew and so did Plato. Herodotus knew. Flannery O'Connor knew how to spin a tale about a one armed Bible salesman from the terrors of the North, just as Nathaniel Hawthorne knew how to spin the yarns of the distaff side, like Hester Prynne, in what amounted to the witchcraft trial a woman was put through with that scarlet letter embroidered, emblazoned on her breast: Adultery. When the sea of heat is smooth as glass, or when the fire burns, to survive there must still be passage whether in skidoos, or fanning oneself down.

Anagrams. A lifelong passion. It was in Alabama I began doing them. So were fire and power. It went deep into the inchoate form of my feminism to picture a woman fire fighter. I didn't have to go south to learn it takes more than sun to make the light shine, especially for girl children.

I realized at last that, divided, born to be torn in half, I stood upon that crack in the earth where the world's light shines. I realized that glass shearing and jack hammering were the human condition reparation where there could be none to our lot. Here in Hades, the stage was being set albeit with minimal props. Here two years beyond the age of reason, and two before puberty, in those Spanish moss and transcending universal darkness, this girl, this child was parting the curtains.

When I was growing up, there were two types girl: Shirley Temple, and Scout Finch. I was definitely Scout Finch in *To Kill a Mockingbird*.

I realized that all those new vests, and sweaters, scarves and stockings did not a new body make. Olympics are held where snow parks have to be created. Bales of hay, scaffolds, providing steps and landings. What one gets is El Niño; weather that changes in a moment. What one wants is a real mind-bending season. That I would get up north again. For now, I bided my time.

We are always saving wildlife photographers from starving to death, brought redemption in the nick of time when they failed to pack enough provisions. We are, at the same time, always driven, tempted to push our brother off the face of the earth. There is always a *Hotel Dieu Grace* hospital in which some woman surgeon is performing a mistaken mastectomy.

Anagrams: *Alabama* spelled *Baa-Lamb* with only one "b" inserted for the beatitudes, the bestiality of this world, the human condition. I realize that I was beginning to speak in the voice of an old woman my seventieth winter, leaving the capes of childhood behind.

We are always doing two-barrel rolls in an airplane, always knocking at heaven's door. It behooves us to always live as though we were on the brink of dying. Little children little problems. Big children big problems. You need moxie in the South.

I perceived that although construction began early, with dump trucks gouging the earth, their huge shovels outlined in fairy lights, the earth could never be cleansed, rethought. Construction was perpetual. Cry eternal.

Far too late workers find a black box from a train collision in Belgium.

I saw indignities against human pride in the way blacks were treated, as I was later to see indignities in the world's treatment of the disabled. Stump they called the boy with one arm. Now is the name of the story. Here comes Stump. He lost the arm as a daredevil, jumping off a moving freight train. We blamed history. We could not ask for blessing for this blame. There was no way when we were that young to measure the thickness of a spine. It was generational like shy cat.

So these tales deal with addiction, forgiveness, prejudgment, incest hinted at and anti-Semitism. Turning back a sheet to rest at night, one finds the blank white reveals a bed redolent of ancestral malaise.

The Union won but the Confederate still dominates to an extent in the South. Just as in New England, watches were exonerated, but republicanism and superstition still rule with a closed fist. Using hyperbole, one could say that the extreme North and the extreme South are, as a lover of mine once said in her first experience of Massachusetts, "Your country is a beautiful grave." In the belles of the South with the schizophrenic behavior of the region with its schisms, one was up against the challenges of chaos and bedlam. In the straight-laced North, one was up against the fusion of the backbone, the ossification that is Puritanism.

Extremity, the polarity that marks a strong country. One saw it in straight laced women in New England, one saw it in righteous women in the South, breasts quivering like a partridge in full courtship dress, woman as round as plump as Ms Couch in Fannie Flagg's masterpiece *Fried Green Tomatoes*.

Alabama broke when I was nine. We didn't' stay long there, on the outskirts of Birmingham, where life was cheap and cheerful if one was poor and happy. Life was austere and sad if one were a person with means. Always, that gaze, mildly admonishing face of Abraham Lincoln looked out at one from the five-dollar bill. Now in my early seventies, I realize that we were indeed at a fork in the road, my tough mama and me, the day when Alabama shattered and gave up the ghost. I realize as well, that this small, intense doll head itself burned with energy. She was the Alabama Light & Power Company.

Morning Glory Jeans

They burned everything but my sun-bleached blue jeans when I was brought into the hospital to die at age twelve and looked around at twilight. The bisque ceramic doll, scotch taped together again, was my highest loss. New Rochelle's tiny cinder block hospital. I remembered the long-legged girl I'd been in the South who always said, "Show me!" living near the Alabama Light & Power Company whose voltage I saw as analogy to our own light and power, as a small reduced family, shrunk by divorce, and to us, that hidden minority, the children. Through whose lips does it speak and drink, Bedlam?

Often they straightened our backs with braces, with Stryker frames which turned the child strapped into a bed like a pancake now in this, now that direction—Reese jackets in extreme cases of curvature of a spine where a rod was inserted and a body cast held the backbone rigid from skull to toes. One was covered like a turtle. A girl's, a boy's face would peek out. Still, we hardly pecked at crumbs. We older kids took up smoking. My own spine was held in a corset with steel bones that cut my shoulder blades and made me think of Lucinda Violet, my aunt's mannequin. She too had no flesh on her bones, picked dry by the blackbirds, uncle would gaffe. These macabre jokes made me laugh in the ward. Without blushing like a peony.

There was a certain milk-blue of morning glory that our jeans had turned. Not deliberately bleached but only by wear and by the sun. This was a color badge we had to earn. Denim mixed with milk paint, squatting, running, climbing. No hiding under a frothy hat for the likes of me.

Once in a while on the ward, rather than being slipped into my ash-rose gingham, or the dotted Swiss, I asked for these jeans, which had by some miracle made it through the fire with my lean twelve-year-old body the night I was stricken. On these star-occasions, which merited a marquee in my book, a Sunday nurse would draw down school attire or street wear from a wire hanger in the metal closets reminiscent of gyms which stood beside each of our hospital cots. On Sundays we were slipped out of regulation hospital gowns and dressed in whatever school clothes we had. Once in a blue moon, I asked for my jeans. The Sunday nurse had a rear end was shaped like the bell of a gourd squash. I was a thin pear. They fit my lean-hipped frame. It was a struggle to fit atrophied hips and rigid spine into the jeans.

These jeans were echoes, mirrors from the summer I had been eleven: faded hollyhock, larkspur and magnolia. I'd climbed the final house frames I was to climb, wearing these jeans.

I'd given my dog away when I pedaled over to the poor part of town and visited Skeezik, named from the comic strip. My dog ended up there because for ten dollars I was commanded by Mother Marcelle to sell him. "He has eight holes in him." He'd got in a fight again and was cowering under our parents' desk—it had belonged to both my parents until the divorcee. This desk had a deep kneehole and tooled gold green leather on top. Mysteriously, and indicting me forever, the first two letters of my name had appeared cut with a letter opener in the right lower hand corner of the Italian leather desk.

How was it that my blue jeans were not burned? All my clothing was when the house was fumigated. It was as if they took the child's flesh but left the skeleton standing... Math tutoring had gone on in these jeans, scouring the country club, which would not allow Jewish people to join. "We'll get even," I incited the other kids and we did, tobogganing over all the nicely sculpted gold ruts when blizzards came. I was light as a grasshopper-kid, the leanest so I rode on the end and always flew off amid gales of laughter.

But with this virus there was no way to get even. A handful, I was not the type of kid who'd carp and grow bitter. I was wiry and still leaping hedges in my heart when I read the headlines from my hospital bed, which spoke of earliest vaccine coming in just the summer I was stricken. We'd jump the great divide between the ill and the well. Mother was standing firm, the ranks were closed. Now I was a hospitalized child but there was another state of mind my imagination lived in.

This state had the hallelujah chorus, the survival meetings along riverbanks and it was my Mecca, the roof I might have jumped off in hospital gown—and flown.

There was no oasis outside. But Mother had given me an accordion file for letters so I could alphabetize all the get-well cards or sympathy notes from schoolmates. I became briefly alarmed. Here was Maggie's card. Here Danielle's. But would I ever see either of those girls again? No kids were allowed to visit: the needle and thread of poliomyelitis had looped through me and I was left untouchable.

Mother got rid of the yellow clock I nightmared over. My nightmare began in the South when we lived next to the Alabama Light & Power Company. In my dream our family sat in a circle. My Forever Family was to change, and the clock circulated like a mythical animal behind us. At whoever's chair it stopped that person would die. I woke up screaming. When I actually came to die, I was silent. No white clock peopled and darkened my dream.

O squandered lambs.

Who was my Forever Family now? A brick incinerator I imaged to be a crematorium stood outside my end of the ward. A desperate dash up the path was made by the dog, Livingstone. He was the exact color of blood pudding. The sky was white as lard, the earth dark as dung. Dark that is, until snow came, sugar powdering bushes, branches, and buildings. I lay on the tilt table 'til my feet burned, itched to run. This was done to stimulate the circulation.

Agnes Peck, my favorite nurse, was in good health, tall and thin with handsome legs, a haunting beauty about her movement, the type I saw coming for me 'til smash bang the virus came and exploded all over me like lit kerosene.

O

Hip-huggers the jeans but boys had ever circled my hips. I was a dirty blond. No Bearington Bears inhabited our world. It was parentless now. Nurses held the way stations. I was a child locked up beside a radiant ocean.

Mother and I used to chase each other round the dining table, I'd shove the table up against the kitchen wall and scoot under. Very few children on the ward were allowed to enter a Griselda mood, which might have occurred among pre-adolescent girls confined. Mother came to the ward once wearing her Beethoven wing collar. Was this to cheer me up? I was envious lying there with budding breasts in my white regulation hospital gown with numbers tamped inside it. I recalled with longing the glory days of our chasing one another round and round the dining table like numerals of a clock now totally ground to a halt, pulverized, ash dust which blew away when I held my palm up to the wind puffing out my cheeks as though blowing a trumpet.

It was dark and late.

No one came, no footfall. The night was lace. Cancerous, riddled. No escape. A dazzling light of being scrutinized was shone upon us children. Every freckle, wart, every curve of bone was seen by hostile eyes. Was it a bit like this in the prison camps? How can we remotely imagine? The shimmering colors swept me away.

That night, when I was lifted out of my jeans I noticed the black and blue mark on my thigh. "How did that get there?" the nurse interrogated.

I did not know. I shook my head.

"Was it the clamps, being measured for braces?"

"I don't know, I told you," I shook my head again.

I went about my conquest in my own way. I could see that she liked me. Blue jeans were passion and hay fields, tall chive grass. She smiled. This passion freed me. I remembered in a flash.

I'd swung myself by one of the bars in the gym, hoisting my skinny body up by my hands last week and had fallen on the exercise mat—in the railroad station cathedral light of the gym in late winter day, early evening, bruising my hip. I didn't feel much then. It was the most dire and extreme hour of all for me, the hour when my whole world view *Weltanschauung* changed. Parents picked up kids but never me. October had come and gone and it was clear that I would not get better to return home with my kin. My Forever Family was changed. No more butterscotch, pencil-smelling schoolrooms with the snap-down maps I adored. The smell of old wooden rulers was still in my nostrils. The kids in the ward were now my block gang. I swallowed hard every Friday that last hour in the gym between four and five. I threw myself to the lions when I dared to lift my slender weight from the mat with my strong (though thin biceps.) Then was when the bruise the size of a grape fruit bloomed. It might have been a boy's hand in rape, my first orgasm behind the barn. But I'd handled that myself too.

"Green eyes," she smiled at me.

It's true that somebody had dubbed them Coke bottle green.

I turned toward the wall.

I would not, could not tell her although a stream of Joycean lyricism came to my inner lips and I must have been close to a grin myself. One of the children had a cancer of the face and the surgeons could not figure how near her right eye it was rooted. This scared me; I saw the branches of innocence wrapped up in the arms of the children. I knew where this fear, however, was rooted, this fear of mine. I missed the hummingbirds back home dipping their needle beaks into red. Did I miss Belle? The world of the schoolroom was never again to be mine. I knew this although the ancient geographies they brought up on carts from the hospital basement made a makeshift schoolroom.

Out of my jeans, I'd realized they felt so good I'd frozen. I'd want to wear them again. Mysteriously, miraculously, to wear them in bed, knees pulled up to chin—I had to do this now with my hand—and burrowing a nose in a book as I had done when a walking child. Now I heard the broken man come.

But now it was the silver wheelchair I wakened to every morning, went to bed every night. "Good night pal, old horse, stallion," I touched the icy silver. It too was the first thing I touched on waking. A..la...bama...cries the long hoot of the freight train under a full moon. My head was spinning. Alabama, you are broken in twain and all your features changed.

What I had wasn't cancer of the spine as I first dreaded. It wasn't spreading but a lace was cast, a narrow net over the body with bowl haircut, heart armoring breaking, cupping each breast in one hand, budding in Ward C bed #9. Jack Frost I was called, "Jacklyn" because I loved painting with words.

I who had taken away peoples' breaths performing Chopin at the music conservatory, I at whom they had gasped because I climbed down fir trees upside down, I was paralyzed and my only claim to fame was that I was having a story "Holly comes home for Christmas," my dream fantasy, published in the *Ward Words* the modest mimeographed publication of the hospital. I never saw the publication.

"You *are* the Alabama Power & Light Company," Mother had said to me once, angrily, when I would not turn out my lights. I was thinking of the *Cassis Rouges* she had bought us in Louisiana where they spoke French and basseted the little bog berries so brightly. I'd rubbed some on my cheeks. I thought of the little lights as these enchanting berries.

○

One night a bridge had broken, a dam had burst. One of the older girls was jackknifed coughing; she had a cigarette cough, at age fourteen no longer little and was crying. If I stopped now, I'd die. Where were the grammars and spellers now? I dreamed of those jeans being taken down, I longed for the stiff cardboard touch of them at first, then the pinafore-tender warmth of them encasing my legs. I lived in a shoebox, there was no tree, no piano, and there might have been drug dealers under my window. The veil was lifted, the ward in water had waves rolling over it, then became very still, mirror-still. I had begun composing stories. Lion heart, I was back in morning glory blue jeans. It was true. From the whip crack, I'd had stardust in my eyes.

Magnolia's Second-Hand Rose

"Our skin sea-planked, / consistent with long light."
    Kathryn Rantala, As If They Were A Basket, Limited First Edition, 2008

Magnolia's was an improvised second-hand clothing shop in the basement of the children's hospital. This all happened over half a century ago. The supervisor who started it was southern, Magnolia Jones, hence its name. She had a little dog at home called Moll for Moll Flanders. She loved that strange book by Defoe about a tart and often regaled the bed-bound kids with tales of Moll.

She'd pull up a chair (not allowed to ruck up a bed) and narrate, "Little Moll stole a chicken wing today..."

The kids would smile, sometimes belly laugh. They didn't' realize then that the heroine was a tart. A little bird would perch outside the ward window in autumn after Moll, the little Yorkshire terrier, died; the little Yorkshire terrier, and magnolia Jones would say, "That's little Moll turned into a bird. Look at her ruffle her feathers."

"Bird's don't have feathers."

The ground in Europe was still smoking from the recently ended war. Magnolia's was a cubbyhole of old wooden closets on wheels jerry-rigged, with scarred and ancient wooden hangers, scarred as magnolia blossom are in the South where Amelia spent her tenth year. Those cream blossoms with small cigarette burns never left her memory. Magnolia's was a series of old cupboards, which rattled, and set in the long corridor between old rehabilitation gym and ancient auditorium. The kids used to joke with each other about going to the Emperor's New Clothes. And they'd strut afterward, hands to hips in new glad rags, the ambulatory kids.

There was nothing regal about the basement of the sanitarium. Childhood traumas of polio, spina bifida and birth defects had left children with deformed hands and paralyzed or spastic fingers which turned over used jeans that had been worn by a walking child.

Amelia's experience with second hand rose began, not down south, where all girls looked like swanked up chickens on Sundays, but rather when she was offered a multi-colored jumper by Kiki's mother. "If Amelia doesn't take it, it goes to the second hand rose," Kiki's mother said.

On the walls of the colonial style Cuthbert home hung one of the Amelia's mother's own oil paintings. "I'm here for my portrait," a child would say who came to Amelia's mother. I'm not here for a handout, she thought but when she ran her hands along the jumper laid out on the bed, the clothing carried the feeling of a human heart having beat behind it.

Amelia was a child of divorce. Her mother sometimes made their supper with her hat still on from the job at a local hosier store. Her mother was tough, she'd been a Grey Lady during the war as her contribution to the war effort. In the war days, when *Buy W.S. War Bonds* signs were stamped on all the post offices, Amelia went to school with a couple of girls who lived in Salvation Army clothes. This dress was floral, and felt buttery. Amelia's mother spread the dress out, patting and smoothing it on the twin bed where the Madame Alexander doll with pink cheeks and blonde sausage curls was propped on a flouncy pillow by day, and said, "It's yours, Amelia, if you want it." It was irresistible in her colors. She was a dark blond, what her mother called dirty blond and she had dark green eyes.

The wind howled over her dolls, Penny Anne and Penny Andy. Pity they would have none. No pity for the South with its honey mouth. Worth for the North stalwart height and light.

By her twelfth summer, the dress would no longer be part of Amelia's wardrobe. The long-waisted frock she inherited from Kiki Cuthbert was passed on to a cousin.

It was during that long hospitalization that clean cuffs on long sleeves shirts made their indelible mark. Her mother would bring one of cousin Micah's old worn boy's shirts from time to time. Paralyzed from the waist down, her legs were so absent that they were a presence everywhere. Her calves had already atrophied, Amelia felt dandy when she wore one of her cousin Ken's shirts. She could almost smell the iron behind them.

By the time a sweetheart saw his unborn children in her eyes, she was not beyond childbearing but he was the wrong man. When she met the right man, he too had been paralyzed, in maneuver ironing in the states when a burning pine tree fell on his spine severing the cord. Devon had no feeling from the waist down.

Over half a century ago, she was stricken. Now this childhood disease was wiped out. "Which bug was that?" taxi drivers asked.

Had that vale of sorrow for children really existed? Amelia succeeded in locating it on a map: she darkened the page with a pencil circle. Children had lain awake at night from screams of bedsores. This was not a painting by Hieronymus Bosch. Hospital records indicate that there was constant patient harm from pressure sores, personnel was deficient, fire exits were severely old fashioned. Furnishing and decorations were inadequate. So were pharmacy services. So what she remembered from fifty-eight years ago she hadn't imagined. Ward life was a nightmare from which one didn't wake. They were real the girls with chestnut hair, nutmeg or cinnamon; real kids with ash blond hair, blond or dove gray eyes, buttery complexions.

She hadn't had time to hug her dog goodbye, nor to take a last look at bicycle and bedroom with her knickknack collection, cherished above all the glass peacock she'd brought back from Georgia, or the blown-glass horse and the swan. A dramatic child, she might have bid *Adieu*. She was borne out one warm July evening off from childhood to an undesignated address.

Instead of leapfrog, there were now wheelchair races which involved the kids whizzing down long tiled hospital corridors. Instead of skinny-dipping in the swimming hole, kids endured soaring temperatures in scalding baths administered in stainless steel Hubbard Tanks. At the age when a 1950's adolescent would be getting high on coke and aspirin, she was on codeine. When she might have cozied low in a plush seat in a twilit Roxie Cinegogue, a boy sheepishly creeping his hand toward her breast or rear, she clenched the therapist's hand against the bone-wrenching pain of bending her spine. Vicariously she experienced romance, listening to whispers between lovers on East River Drive. She had slipped her hand into an imagined lover along the warm and breezy summer drive, twelve years old and twelve stories below the big city hospital window. Instead of a prom dress, she was brought a wheelchair, one of the old wooden ones, a relic from the war.

Little-by-little that summer outside all time, of 1951, she was being transformed into another child, another girl. It was like the South: time stood still. She read about mirror-neurons and imagined winking mirrors in merry-go-rounds.

○

Downtown Manhattan in winter, covered in snow resembled a baroque fairy tale when she was brought home form the hospital after half a year. She was not yet thirteen. The art deco Chrysler building, the turn-of-century brownstones, the wire-cut brick, all held snow with mystery and a touch of the old world. Once back home, there were oil paintings hung on the West 73rd brownstone, with marble foyer and curved brownstone apron stoop she learned to climb on crutches and long leg braces. Her mother had set up the typewriter, the old Royal Underwood, its dots, circular black keys hard to press. Frogs in flashlight leapt on pajamas echoed by those she found at the second-hand rose in the hospital basement.

Amelia didn't expect it, but there was a constant ache in her chest: she missed the hospital gang. She had a dream of blue jeans which had the fly in front had once belonged to some boy. The hole in the wall sold clothing to kids for a nickel. These were children starved for outdoor clothing. Some of the clothing had been bought from retailers in near new condition, some given by parents who could afford designer clothing for their children who had little life ahead for them. For mobile shoppers, secondhand clothing bought at a second hand rose can be near mint condition, but for bed-bound children, a tatty old scarf will do. "We gotta take you to Magnolia's," one of the older kids would say, and drag a limping child by the hand. Most of them knew the story of the emperor's new clothes. But these were not clothes for children.

Was she still a child? The same thing happened to her in the ward that had happened at camp her last year walking: there was an overflow and she was singled out as the mature one. It was on the long train ride from Manhattan to the Adirondacks that she had coveted the prospect of being in the sub-senior's bunk a second year: she cherished the rooms, the wood on the walls, the views from that bunk's window. On the train, an older girl had been informant, older by only two months. "One of the kids is being farmed out to seniors."

"Who?" Amelia asked

"You."

It happened in the South too where she grew up too sudden, the South where girls wore hair ribbons big as country churches, and misbehaving was acting ugly. The most grown-up of the sub-seniors could fit in with the eldest girls in the camp, the director had figured. The lump in her throat began to grow wings like a baby bird inside her shell. When she got off the train, her counselor came up, checking her from head to toes, and said, "I love your smile."

She was raging inside, beating child fists against the walls. "You get the bunk at the edge of the forest," the girl who was agent wound up the news. It's true; there were night sounds, owls and bats audible from that dark outer ring.

She began drawing a loose-leaf sized page map. This is what Kathryn-Amelia did whenever her imagination had to create an escape. She did this during the actual war, when she hadn't heard her parents argue but she had absorbed the repression and depression clinging to walls like Spanish moss down in the deep South. That year, at age nine, she had constructed a little drawer with cups and saucers which pulled out from her parents' wardrobe and which she set for the dolls' tea. Those were nicotine-colored afternoons in which the magnolia, cream with their small nicotine burns, opened and wafted their sweet-sick fragrant through the grayish air.

Tonight, on the eve of her seventh decade, she took the black mock-fur jacket she'd brought home from ladies' wear on approval yesterday. She carefully eased the jacket off its store hanger padded with satin and laid it out on the bed. She wore her silver hair in the same boy bob she'd had when she wore those scratchy hospital gowns, when she snuck her first quick grabs in the hallways from her wheelchair. The older kids taught her. And took her first lung drags of a cigarette. "I am a fallen woman," she whispered to Albina, her cubicle mate, and a thalidomide disaster born with flipper hands.

Once upon a time, a very long time, there was an emperor. And this emperor owned so many fancy clothes that he could have supplied everyone at a very big Halloween party with a costume! The emperor received merchants from around the world who offered him fancy fabrics, silks and satins... But one day, three gentlemen arrived with a fabric so magical that it had to remain top secret!

○

She and her mother had once lived in the South, the year they moved to establish residency in Georgia which was one way to obtain the divorce. The only ground for divorce in 1948 in the northeast was adultery with photographs for proof. Her mother epitomized the iron claw in the velvet glove. They had been those Shakespearean lilies that festered and stank far worse than weeds. During childhood and all throughout Amelia's recovery she and her mother had been inseparable. Amelia gradually gained some independence and somewhat broke the bonds of braces and crutches growing into a peculiar tormented womanhood. They jumped on the other's last nerve until they brokered a temporary truce, a *modus vivendi*. After a moral drubbing, what record exists of a repentance? There is something eerie and haunting about emotions and settings, which are changeless. Ironically, they change the color of things, chairs in a room; they provoke intractable pain.

"I want my mama! I want my mama," cried the child at the end of the ward still a baby, Kitty Kramer, aged two admitted for orthopedic surgery thus kept in the cubicle closest to the nurse's station. Nobody on the ward slept that night. Amelia recalled, *I had never heard this sound before, I slipped down a wormhole of time, and it was an Iowa Waltz. I saw the fields of corn in that child's cornflower blue eyes. I saw the hands of a garden angel holding ash petals.*

Mrs. Kuchenbrock, the night nurse, was dainty and silver-haired and came and went to the adenoidal chant of the bereft child. She had a heart-rending discipline. That backbone of iron, one sensed, was bought at a price higher than pearls or rubies. Peacock child Amelia had become, changing colors, flaring a vivid tail (telling an even more vivid tale). She brought herself ecstasy, the white light, at late hours of the highly regimented hospital afternoon. A boy would have said, "I played with my snake. I began rising."

○

During the night of Kitty's rage and grief, a quiet moment had come when all the beds in the ward turned cobalt blue as though radiated. It was a bit like turning a radio to lowest volume. The silence was deafening. Then Kitty had filled her lungs with air increasing, pitch, intensity, and volume of her cries. It was as though a fire burning in the little cot at the end of the ward, a blaze which no water could put out and all the children were ignited as though the fire leapt, all were burning at once with this afflicted infant. It was like a flood whose wave had a great undertow, which undertow lifted, pitched all of them until they were forced to face imminent and certain death: the broken man had come.

"Helpless one!" the stern subordinate night nurse shook her finger at Albina who had rung and rung for the night nurse. "You wet yourself."

It was better than, "You shat yourself," but Albina was left in wet sheets the night.

Amelia would exit the ward by fantasizing a trip to Magnolia's. She closed her eyes, lay under the hospital sheets but began trying on all the closets garments, Magnolia's. She tried on a grey velour hat which she dreamed up like a confection, tilted it at an angle which made her wildly rakish, and stylish like Greta Garbo at an airport meeting some soldier boy, lighting up a cigarette. This hat and her chin up-tilted in lamplight showed off the velveteen crush rose and the slightly noble Roman profile she had as a young woman. Hers was an intensely orchestrated hospital life: entrances, exits, and curtains.

○

The final argument is one we cannot win. It is with death. During war there was wet laundry strung across a clothesline in the military base kitchen, slapping one in the face. Amelia tiptoed across the kitchen, ducking from damp underclothes and sheets, waving her arms like a scarecrow to beat back the wet white towels and the beige translucent stockings but they always won and slapped her in the face.

What does one do when one has the answer on the other side of the door?

That once or twice Amelia had worn Kiki's velvet frock, she had felt she wore something foreign to her. When the white hospital gown became her garb in the harsh atmosphere. It was her own.

It is sad to remember bliss on a ward. She remembered the precise moment when she stood—aware even then of the joy in long limbs—on the small hill in suburban post war New Rochelle where she'd realized that to become aware of another happiness, one about to come, in the midst of a present happiness was a peak experience. She lived among Christian muscular children whose parents reared them with Puritan standards. She was a pariah, an Ishmaelite, a wiry delicate Holbein Jew.

"You were born to be torn in half," her mother commented. She did not remember the exact moment when she exchanged one body for another. But she knew it had taken place when she looked into the mirror at her body in a wooden wheelchair with hoop wheels, not the tall slim girl of twelve she had grown into through many summers exercising tree- climbing grace, rope-climbing, racing to beat the boys, slamming her girl body, eleven years old, all ninety-one pounds, hand on the wall of the gym to catch her weight. She was the fastest runner of them all.

The boy of seven who had to give up his dog pulled back the dog's ear flap to whisper, "You and I are not getting along, fella, we must give the other up." So she felt toward her girlhood, the part when she was a child and could still walk. Further back than that Alabama who shattered, her power, her light snuffed out to all but a flicker guttering where a power company had been.

When she took home the first jacket for her seventieth birthday, it was a possibility, then all wrong. But she had worn it round the house in her wheelchair and in an impulsive moment had taken the tags off. She returned it.

"The cuffs are soiled," said the shop woman who had agreed over the phone to take the jacket back.

Amelia felt vilified. "May I try this on?" she asked, holding up another jacket, white with cornflower blue embroidering.

"Alright. But do not even turn around in it; the cuffs are white on this one too."

Cuffed, Amelia two weeks shy of seventy, felt chastised, a child made to stand on one foot in the corner of the classroom. It was heady, was her wine, the emperor's new clothes. All of a sudden that cupboard of a second hand rose in the hospital basement flashed back: she saw in a vision of Magnolia's. It was an epiphany: in one moment. Lit up were dusty black velvets and cords of gray: each image, cupboard, coat with tears, tatty jacket, boy's jeans was like a glass knife cutting her. While the shop woman's jaw continued moving up and down, Amelia was able to push the shop woman's face closed like a cupboard with two doors. Now, although the entrepreneur was bustling, shredding one receipt, making out another, she was become invisible to Amelia in the seventy-year-old woman's eyes.

She knocked at the doll maker's shop. But the doll maker was not home.

She lifted the boiled wool jacket with blue mock-Tyrolean embroiders out of rustling frosty hothouse-type tissue. "It's boiled wool, isn't it?" she had asked the shopkeeper, one last question.

"Yes."

"Can you wash or only dry clean?"

"Dry clean."

There appeared to be a moment's hesitation at Country Life. "Would that stop you from taking it home and trying it? She smiled glancing at the tell tale cuffs. Handicap is the gift that goes on taking, Amelia thought.

"No." Today she slipped it over her shoulders and hugging careful not to let a cuff brush a silver wheel, not to maul the cuffs. She felt like an actress stiffening her backbone, drawing herself to her height: *I am here for my portrait, I can begin to speak a line*, she decided. She was, people said, terrific, tender, a presence. It too was wrong. That was when she sprang for the black, which worked.

Her birthday would come and go in two week's time to break up the soap-white dull of winter. The woman had said, "I don't care what you do with it after you buy it, you can do anything you like, but don't get dirt on those boiled white cuffs before you actually lay your money down. I need to be able to sell it again."

She held forth her hand with only a thorn-burn of light visible, a stigmata, like the rope burn left by the rope she'd climbed fifty-eight winters ago in the New Rochelle public primary school gymnasium.

She breathed with pain in the blue in the thin, potato light of a February afternoon. There was no playhouse to clamber into, no small store from which to choose goods. She was staying a course, that there were things up for grabs, albeit muted ones. Muted and mute, the objects stood about her. How could it be only three in afternoon? Amelia is preparing for a night flight. She could neither waltz nor wheel about the room in this new garment which became immediately a coat of hope.

"Pleasure," said Robinson Jeffers, "is the carrot dangled to lead the ass to market or the precipice." Are there carrots here, in this dark light, Amelia wonders. The ward has left no one to tell the story. Yet there is me. I have never experienced the river, bathing nude in the river since age eleven. I am experienced but have never experienced the wedding gown, thought Amelia crossing the midnight sea to Europe, wearing the caftan of melancholy quite like before. Before. The body is a house: it has windows, and chimney, which is silent or roars: but the body has no doors.

By her twelfth summer, the dress wouldn't do in her world. "Were the lilies that stink far worse than weeds," she'd paraphrased Shakespeare the night of her agony. Amelia, she would be paralyzed from the waist the long waist and elegant skirt of the jumper she inherited from Kiki Cuthbert passed on to a cousin.

Hallucinatory, alabaster, the hospital children. Haunting. If she could enter one of their bodies and exit her own whom would she choose? Leila Rifkin who had twisted hands and feet and had wanted to be a ballerina? Albina born with thalidomide flippers for hands at the shoulders? No. She would choose her own all over again. For the pitch, the roller coaster ride, the ecstasy, the pain. Her mother had early inured her to pain. She had a little Moll but his name was Skadoo. She was made to give him away at age eleven and sold her dog for ten dollars. Just like that. No time for tears.

In this chiaroscuro existence, she had died and come back again. "Shut your face," the teacher down south would say. She was wilting on the vine. Those mirror-neurons, however functioning. In the South girls wore hair ribbons bigger than a country church and kept their legs together, as best friends. Misbehaving was acting ugly.

Lynn Strongin

The night I died I was twelve years old. I did not rise from my body in the E.R. No, instead, what I did was I stepped through an almost translucent wall. Now I am a revenant, come back. It was then that these always starched, always vellum-colored long clean cuffs, smelling of scorch and steam on shirts her mother would bring from time-to-time from Micah cut their deepest impression. Atrophied legs were daily growing thinner, emaciated as she was helped by the nurse first to put one art and then the other through the sleeves, she felt dapper, almost robust again. She saw the triangular burn of the scorch-birds in the ironing board her mother had sprung out vehemently back home. Lilies that fester smell far worse than weeds. The scorch birds brought back the South to her, the cigarette burns magnolia blossoms have. These shirts were flawless as fresh-fallen snow when it is whipped cream.

She missed winters. Autumns. Summers. Springs. Paralysis had eaten up all her seasons that year and left a glittering world of echoes and mirrors. She missed butterscotch schoolrooms, snap down maps which were glossy, the raisiny smell of the pencil box the first day of classes and the Scrip inkwells sunk into desks. She missed rulers, turn-of-century brick the color of old roses. But in Micah's shirt she felt dandy, jazzed.

This all happened over half a century ago. The supervisor who started it was southern, Magnolia Jones, hence its name. She had a little dog at home called Moll for the infamous tart. She regaled bed-bound kids with tales of Moll. She'd pull up a chair or bend over an ear and begin, "Little Moll stole a chicken leg today …"

The kids would grow round-eyed. She closed her eyes. She could always almost smell the burn of the steam iron behind cotton.

Hawk's Eye View of a Buxom English Teacher

We know absolutely nothing about the appearance of the Celestial Stag (maybe because nobody has ever had a good look at one), but we do know that these tragic animals live underground in mines and desire nothing more than to reach the light of day. They have the power of speech and implore the miners to help them to the surface. At first, a Celestial Stag attempts to bribe the workmen with the promise of revealing hidden veins of silver and gold; when this gambit fails, the beast becomes troublesome ...
    Jorge Luis Borges, Book Of Imaginary Beings

For Kay Boyle, Poet, Teacher, and Friend
Berkeley June 1972—Victoria Spring 2009

The Drive Down Coast: Sarne and Lee

Seven silver ducks moved on the pond: they were in the water of her memory, when she was very young, could walk, and spent summers in Peekskill at her grandfather's estate.

"What was I like then?" she asked her younger sister, Alma.

"You couldn't be contained."

She could remember the brilliance of those summer days, the elation in a body moving as if at some divine command—legs, arms thin as wands, sun-bronzed, spinning her in cartwheels over grass, back flips, headstands. There weren't enough ways she could express her *joie de vivre*.

Now Sarne, twenty-nine (but looking ten years younger), was thin, under 100 pounds, about five-foot-four, wore two sweaters, hunched in the rider's seat opposite the tall blonde Lee and whispered to herself, *Sweet Jesus! Make our reunion good! Parting will be hell!*

Lee is motoring them down the Oregon coast for a one-night getaway before Sarne packs off for the Arizona desert where she will not always be cold. She wears desert boots, ironically, over her feet because with paralyzed legs poor circulation is a given. Lee drives in silence for long patches in the teeth of the wind. She's been packing Sarne off for the desert.

"You're wearing two sweaters again, Kiddo," Lee laughed from the wheel. Sarne wore two sweaters, button to the neck, two-color wool showing at her wrist, brown and blue.

"Don't let me forget the skewers for the broils. When I stop at the supermarket for steak.

Lee, pushing forty, rising five foot ten, hefty, dark blonde with bangs, laughed again, "Been too busy to cross myself."

She bore her 180 pounds well, head held high, with musical voice, quick to laugh, slow to anger. She had an enormous capacity for work, and strode rather than walked.

Sarne needed no help transferring from wheelchair to Lee's kicky brass-bright Triumph, although Lee held the handles and packed the chair easily in the orange trunk. This was to be their hiatus in the chaos of packing: twenty-four hours together on the ocean in a friend's loaned cabin. Lee wore waffle-stompers.

"I've been busy as a one-toothed mouse in a room of cheddar," Sarne laughed, in a high voice, which was like south-sweet corn Lee claimed. In her hands Sarne turned a piece of drift glass Lee had gathered for her from the beach last evening; blue green, polished on one side, Lee said it was storm-glass.

Lee has features composed as a mask often, using language for hedge, and intellect as defense; although at times, relaxed. Lee's craggy face can be a strong register for emotion.

"You look tired, kiddo," she said, darting Sarne a sidelong glance from the wheel, and added, "You'll be getting out of it all soon."

Sarne went on smiling, looking down at the glinting storm-glass, giving it a Madonna smile.

Sarne could imagine Lee riding a horse; wearing jodhpurs, top-hat, and an elegant silk scarf tied at the neck, very swish and riding boots. But Lee had never ridden a horse a day in her life despite coming from the Midwest, Minnesota.

"You're the one I picture riding. Whippersnapper, horsing that chair around 'til it could almost nay."

The chair was put out as Quickie. Sarne dreamed wings.

Evening fog was closing in, making it necessary to switch the head lamps on. Sarne remembered the last evening she'd walked, at age twelve. The virus was already in her spinal cord, burning out the connection between spine and limbs: her legs were becoming more and more leaden. She'd forced herself to walk to the doorway, even though the doctor had forbidden her to; he was downstairs talking with her mother; it felt as though a ball and chain were tied about her ankle; fever running up and down her spinal column, her backbone on fire it felt like, her legs knives buckling. But she took the journey from bed, wringing wet sheets she'd tried to sleep in the night before; she forced herself to rise in order to hug Alma goodbye. Now, that was long, long ago…she leaned her head back against the car-seat, closed her eyes, hearing the car lap up the miles. She shrugged. The ache in her shoulders.

Silver Wheels was another of Lee's nickname, but she called her Kiddo most often. Sarne opened her eyes. Lee had been far slimmer two years ago when they met at a conference for college English teachers. She'd worn a grey print scarf, tailored suit, one chrysanthemum in a buttonhole.

"You often wear blue, Lee, or green. You're a sea-person if ever there was one. I'll take me a fill of this," Sarne waved to the ocean, "before hitting Phoenix."

Lee flicked the windshield wiper on, had a sudden desire to punch the lighter button in; she'd quit the weed but the desire to start up again dogged her.

"You'll not miss this, m'dear!" Lee chortled. "You'll be where you can bake out. Aye."

"Aye. Write?"

"You know me, I'm no letter writer."

She knew Lee. Felt dizzy when she closed her eyes again recalling the one dozen cartons of books they'd packed over the past ten days.

Born, raised a Mennonite, Lee had been baptized a Dunkard, unconsciously controlled by discipline, as native to her as her heartbeat. She recoiled from poems of desire for she claimed they betrayed the Mona-Lisa smile of self love.

"How's the article coming?" Sarne asked.

"Like molasses in January. A sentence at a time. My Overview of the College English Teacher."

"What'll you call it?"

"Don't know yet."

Sarne thought of "Hawks eye view of a Buxom English Teacher."

"Let's face it, Lee: you have an analytic mind, you love to pick the meat from the bone. You're a cross between—an intellectual and a bohemian."

"You're quick as Jack Frost."

"Ha! Not with these purple rings under my eyes," she laughed, flipping the windshield mirror in front of her down, sticking her tongue out at herself, flipping it back. She was fine-boned, thin, hair shaped in the feathered cut of an Italian boy bob: light red-brown, it turned blond in bright sun. When she'd had a bout with pain—like now—she had ashen rings under her eyes making her look older than her twenty-nine.

"Like Emily, you're no mild-mannered, woman," Lee retorted, "The fire will come out in your writing."

O

They stood in sharp contrast to each other: Lee's features were craggy, rough-hewn; Sarne had an oval face lightly freckled, and still bore traces of the pallid girl she was when stricken at age twelve: a Modigliani girl, but auburn, with asymmetrical features. Whereas Lee was a Netherland painter's woman, a glad girl nearing forty—ruddy, full of rude energy and devotion, with high coloring, Sarne was olive-skinned, with a straight, slightly Roman nose.

Strapping, Lee wore clothes with reckless style. Sarne wore a blue cardigan over a brown pullover. About ten years apart, both were college English teachers fond of Irish wools, thick homemade soups, Mulligan stews. Lee laughed about her deli taste. Lee was Amish, Sarne unorthodox Jew. Lee Midwestern, Sarne, New Englander.

Sarne punched in the lighter, pulled a cigarette out of her hip pocket.

"Whoa, kiddo" Lee said, "A girl who's been in a lung."

"I told you, Lee, the lung was in my room but I never needed it."

The lighter popped and Sarne grabbed it, its orange star glowing in the late afternoon like an ember.

They were lighthouse buffs, seafood enthusiasts. All their dates were on the water.

At ten on a Sunday morning, Lee would arrive, like Nancy Drew in her roaster, a knight on white horse, and sport them off for six hours by the ocean, starting out with a brunch of scrambled eggs, bacon and gin at Tiburon Tommy's on Shale Cove. In the strong morning light, Lee's eyes were jade, like the ring she wore on her left hand, which her father, a stonecutter, had made her. Ruggedly handsome, windbreaker collar up, long hands turning wine glasses by their stems. Or holding a mug of cold beer on draft, dark blonde cut in a shag.

On those rare occasions when they drove no where but visited in Sarne's Berkeley living room, Sarne walked up and down and talked. She never stopped striding.

It had been a weird winter. Gunmetal grey days had come in droves, the sky had opened, unzipped, and poured buckets at the time she and Lee began to see one another. Sarne had to quit her teaching post in a prep school for lily white rich girls because of an accumulation of fatigue, and pain. Was this the dread post-polio syndrome? Lee helped pay for treatments to stretch Sarne's spine.

They became lovers of each other's spirits early on. Do lovers often ease their own loneliness at the price of breaking with their world?

Blacks kept being thrown in jail that spring. Angela Davis had said, "No solidarity without suffering." All our suffering is historical, thought Sarne: the war, my polio; of one place, one time, located in its set notch in history. A war is ended overnight. A disease made extinct.

○

Who was the sterner sister between them? Lee's temper and genius were protective coloration.

Goodbye, Lee, she would have to say soon. Next week.

Goodbye, she rehearsed as they drove the last ten miles. *Your soul must be compassion. This is not the end of the play—but it is the end of the act. My house was in a state of war this winter: my mother returning, the endless rain, highs—but only from painkillers. My illness seeming to recur. You saw me through—and now you are seeing me off.*

Lee turned to look at Sarne at a stoplight.

"Hey, kiddo, you've already looked the old devil in the face!"

"And you overcame your background."

"Me? Let's face it: I come from a dead mining town," Lee began, "I mean, not far from the Mason-Dixon Line in Ohio. It was all bricked-in factories which held gloom like a mother. I was a middle child, sandwiched between two boys, ruled by a strict father. Believe it or not, Sarne, I wore kid gloves, and actually carried alligator bags in the fifties."

Did Lee know that to Sarne this speech about daily life was a blessing?

"Tell me more."

"Well, you know I went to a Baptist college in the Midwest."

"And you grew into a clean Pennsylvanian-Dutch, raised Amish, Pacifist," Sarne finished.

"Perhaps. But did you know I wanted to go to an eastern women's college?"

"Why didn't you?"

"My Father put his foot down, said *No!* But let me tell you, I did the dances and sororities; my younger brother called me his all-American beauty at age twenty, and you wouldn't believe me, Sarne, standing five-foot-ten on deck of the family boat."

"You got to do the stuff that polio spared me."

"You could see it like that. I needed to strike out on my own."

"So what did you do?" Sarne exhaled, and ground out the stub of her cigarette in the car ashtray.

"So I moved west, took my real estate boards, had a bunch of snazzy real estate cards printed up looking like Carol Channing in *Guys & Dolls*, and sold real estate in my twenties until I decided teaching must be my true calling. So I returned to college at age twenty-six, took a Master's in English and found a position in a private school for girls. I adored kids, always motoring one or another to or from school. I'd tell these kids, 'Forget about your mother's fur-coats. Look about the land! It's spring. The sheep are lambing like balls of dust upon Bible green Oregon hills the baby lambs hung.'"

○

Still, one way Lee didn't cut the cheese with the administration; she got chewed out by the headmaster for not wearing hose.

She took to saying, "It's not for nothing the Lord gave me broad shoulders." She downed one-fifty of rye some evening now, her blue-grey eyes were bloodshot.

She's the Celestial Stag, Sarne thought. Because she lives underground in a basement apartment with grilled windows, gas range littered. Because it's an obstacle course to get to her telephone. Because the light of day seldom penetrates the gloom. Because she's held by the power of language, probing hidden veins of gold and silver.

They engaged in literary conversation. The hawk's eye view.

Sarne said, "I've been reading Gertrude Stein, *Picture of Occupied France*. You like Stein?"

"*Like* her! When I was in college my pal and I cut our hair like Steins, we dressed like Gertrude Stein, we read her aloud for hours. We *were* Stein."

Sarne picked up the thread, "Stein says that 1939 was a marvelous raspberry year. You know, that's the year I was born. End of the dirty thirties. Lice kept making jam. Stein kept walking Basket the Second, their dog. Just like nothing was happening, like Europe was not about to cave in, she and Alice continued trimming boxwood hedges, making jam. Let me read you what I've jotted down for my article, "Psychological Ragtime."

She drew an article out of her tote on the car floor, which held a sheaf of writing.

Gradually, there were no more Sundays. April was nearly over. Tuesday began. German attacks, General Weygand. It certainly was no longer pleasant. Then May. Listen to the radio. Walk the dog. Make the dam. Close the shutters. Plug the ears. Here come the cannons. Color of brimstone. Green-yellow. German Soldiers arrive in hordes in the French provincial towns. The Occupation. Eating sweets and anything that looked like champagne. Buying their women silk stockings. Stein goes on reading the Prophecies. And it all comes so. Alice Toklas makes the soldiers chocolate cakes and socks. Then the question arose of gasoline and butter. Finally they manage to get that. Then all thoughts turn to peace. The French agreed there was good after all. They were becoming soft. War came along to challenge them.

"Ha!" Lee laughed. "The whole history of intrigue. People feel women create intrigues to stave off the boredom of their lives. Some feel there would be no war in a world of women. But, midyear, men do cry themselves to sleep: I have brothers, I know. Those are my thoughts, but read me more?"

"O.K." She read again in a musical voice, lowering in pitch:

Do women take out revenge upon their own bodies? Since it does seem necessary to avenge ourselves in order to maintain the emotional balance of life. Do they not make of daily living a consoling religion? One thinks in terms of milk delivery, gasoline, the sale of pigs. One goes on reading the prophecies, like Stein.

"Sarne, listen: To get back to my article, the great heft of scholarship has been behind the strict approach to writing. But more and more I find wherever I am, I turn out to be the generative force, not the imitative one. We've got to give something to students to bring back love of the language."

"Absolutely. I've always been an Ishmael. We've got to know the Ishmael, the misfit inside-out."

"But, look here, from Tristan Shandy on, the queer has been the work of the joyful, always."

"Yes!"

"And George Eliot is far and away the deepest psychologist. Look how she probes human nature! By large-spirited and pitying brush strokes. Look how Adam Bede opens, mid-December..."

"I know," said Sarne, "with a Methodist preacher-woman in 1850 before a hushed, expectant audience."

"Exactly. I love the beginning of Adam Bede."

"But you know what one critic says about Jane Austen's last work *Persuasion*? He says that to become bookish is a very last salvation. He says Austen had the maturity of one loyal to her own values. That in such a compact world, romantic love becomes a disruption."

"It can," interjected Lee.

"But he says Jane Austen knows other forms of insulation in our close society are falsehood, and polite lies."

"Indeed."

The question Sarne was asking herself as she quoted the critic was, "Did Lee see herself being civilly false, politely evasive?"

"The thing is Lee, that neither person breaks off by viewing the other clinically. The drawing room was the usual role."

It was comforting to read this historical insight into Lee, but it might have been wrong. It was soothing to become a somewhat old fashioned girl with those virtues.

"Lee, it was even a solace when I graduated to become a woman going for her Ph.D. although college grads used to josh when I graduated Hunter 'Petticoat-Hanging-Down' is followed by M.R.S."

"I still see Austen," Lee was vehement, "as victim of the establishment whereas George Eliot—ho! She broke out on her own. Her conviction of the dignity and pathos of human life My God, she's so popular because of her full-boded pictures of country life."

"She's' a countrywoman."

"But of course. Look at her joy in creating atmosphere. I feel none of that gusto, Sarne, in your Jane Austen. I'm sorry, kiddo, but you can keep that tight-lipped moralist."

"You exaggerate, always."

"Eliot," Lee was ecstatic, flushed by this time—they were almost there, "she has such affection and energy. I absolutely revel in her gusto."

"I know. But let me tell you this about my Austen—"

"She had a fast love for the fact. Right. Head and shoulder above Austen, Eliot. That's what she did was to celebrate the worth of the commonplace life!"

They'd reached their destination.

Getting out of the car, Sarne said, "You realize, Virginia Woolf died of being a woman."

Lee was silent and shuddered.

○

Entering the cottage—straight out of *Lady Chatterley's Lover*, it struck Sarne—flipping her chair easily over the lintel Sarne thought, Lee's so radiant but in the act of running away, vivid in running. Not like her, borne down by years of struggle, but her lip was buttoned, high as the top button of her trench coat collar. I remember Lee was born in Ohio, south of the Mason Dixon line. She was taught nice girls don't touch. Was taught "acting ugly" was mean manners in church where she wore a hair ribbon big as that country church. I was a Jew born in the Northeast, raised partially and crucially in the South with its particular song and stain.

Was there something Lee found magnetic about *Sarne?* Overly thin, with traces of illness, but vibrant, her breasts like small firm oranges under her sweaters? She wrote stories examining the way history muffed it for women, which reflected Lee's own urgent need to make herself free. At times, when the shot rang too close to home, bullet would glance bone, Lee would jump.

"I paint a picture, and lose a friend," Sarne would say echoing John Ruskin. So Sarne learned to keep her insights to herself.

Lee herself realized that when it came to putting these principles Sarne perceived into her own life, her thirty-nine years were stacked bitterly against her. Each year a slab of firedog for burning, but she could not quite bring herself to burn them. She stood at the edge.

Sarne was fascinated by what survives, and loved to listen for echoes of what didn't survive. When she was a young child, she kept the paper instructions that came with her uncle's tools and deliberately scrunched and mistreated them: rubbed them in dirt until they resembled, in her child eyes, some immensely valuable, secret document which had fallen into her hands. That was the birth of her love affair with words. Something from her revered uncle was there to divine and thereby connect with him if only she could work the connection out.

The need, Sarne intuited, in Lee to cross the threshold was what drew her most strongly to Lee. This and her own diving desire for shelter, to be taken as she'd never been, however roughly, under somebody's wing.

Lee was a Puritan, some ways but not in drinking: glass upon glass, a bright burning, a slow dying.

Sarne found it hard to recognize Lee some evenings.

She thought to herself, is it because I'm myself living in the dusky twilight of pain—that I bear this? Something rapt in Lee's holding back gives forth. She suffers me by going into the dark, then throwing out pulses. I would practice Bach in the clear light of morning but I bear this muting instead. I must tear these cobwebs form my brain. It is I who have lost touch with true breathing... having to content myself with less, like a nun in a convent.

If Lee was bold colors, Sarne was Giotto's colors, delicate shadings in the canvas, perhaps they did make a painting: war implied, but simply two humans living with the taste of peace yet not the full condition.

"We must realize society denied our mothers expression of humor, along with much else," Lee said, handing Sarne some plastic plates from the cabinet. We didn't need the South to get warm. Sarne set them out, blowing dust off them.

"But a complex, beautifully organized library?" Sarne raised her eyebrows, smiling.

"O.K. Kiddo, we're both Jane Austenites like our mothers before them, in desiring great shelves of books. Both gave in, Sarne to pressures of a social milieu which heightened their personal isolation. Each saw herself as devoted teacher, dutiful daughter."

"So maybe all their stories and poems, turned out to be variants of the Cinderella story?"

"The foundling princess, yes!"

Sarne took the bottle of chilled wine Lee handed her. "Emotional foundlings." She realized she'd always felt like a foundling. It was salty and rural here, she thought, as she noticed the oak beamed ceiling, the delicate floral print, warped by water, in the niche off the kitchen. How nice it would be to be at an outdoors French restaurant being served chilled wine wrapped in a white napkin, sunlight making the golden Chablis sparkle...

Humans can create mystery, but they cannot control it.

Lee was sautéing jumbo shrimp in the wok as an appetizer. At times their relationship reminded Sarne of a British mystery. She could hear their dialogue in clipped British accents. She watched *The Hound of the Baskervilles* for the fifth time last night on the midnight screen. There they were, she and Lee. Sherlock and Watson. That dashing pair, running across English lawns in their flowing cloaks, hiding more than half of themselves. But the pair kept missing the hound. At precisely ten o'clock, one would take his leave to cross the moor.

Sarne thought that Lee, like Anne in Jane Austen's last novel, *Persuasion*, improbably brought her chief misfortune upon herself through a mistaken deacons: Lee went to put on an l.p. of *The Mamas and The Papas*, letting worldly wisdom outweigh love, an error forgiven in the mature Cinderella's mother, more ragged.

"You are my social life," Lee reached across the table taking Lee's hand.

"And you mine," Sarne bowed.

That social life is life, both women knew. They knew that for Austen what could be seen governed the world. *What one person in a community enacts is seen by the rest.* Hence Lee, living in the Haight-Ashbury, commuting to her job down the peninsula. Lee, perhaps forgoing what she must surely hold highest in the scale of values—love—in order to hold onto her worldly position. One's kingdom for a horse. That was, if she was a closet case, as Sarne had believed all along.

In the cottage like the gamekeepers in Britain, they fell to, over shrimps. And the idea turned, midair, to catch Sarne. For was it not more noble to renounce personal joy in order to fulfill a role as teacher, say, in the world? Or was Lee's presumed choice simply a matter of mending her psyche, holding body and soul together?

"Women do have the unenviable privilege, m'dear, of loving longest when existence or hope is gone."

They fell silent for a few moments while Sarne entertained vivid pictures of Austen in those nearly impenetrable grays shot through by a shaft of golden light: the linsey-woolsey of Austen's moral fiber, her roles to mother and aunt...the image came bright upon her optic nerve. She considered Woolf who went about laying networks of relationships with care. She went on digging gardens. Still, all rent apart at the iron thumb of war. A sense of attrition had entered the human mind. Woolf had to endure two wars. She's right in her 1928 masterpiece *A Room Of One's Own*, right in all regards, and in these three major ones—a woman needs money and a room of her own, because money is necessary for time, and time for happiness, and romance had been annihilated by seeing our brothers' faces in light of shellfire. Our capacity for the mouth opening in the ecstatic sigh—had been killed forever.

What I really want to say is that I love her—Sarne thought. I see her inability to deal with her own emotions and love her nonetheless. I thought of that southern flick *The Last Picture Show*.

○

Yes, thought Sarne, confirming her earlier impression: we have entered a cottage right out of Lady Chatterley's Lover, the gamekeeper's woman, a quarter mile from the ocean.

They could hear surf rolling in and crashing as they consumed the shrimp. It was now dark, past twilight. Lee's trench coat was tossed on the sofa. Sarne kept her cardigan and pullover sweaters both on, periodically giving a tug to the one that extended below the cuff of the cardigan. *Writing, she thought, was mainly pain.* This evening by the sea would be a relief however the dice were cast. The room felt rocked by the waves, but she could not rock to oblivion the memory of her evenings incarcerated with pain. Lee was filled with nervous energy, drawing skewers for broils from the oven. Sarne, being thin, felt the cold easily.

Worse, she'd recently begun to experience *the fear* again. There was *the white light* and then *the fear*. She'd known both since childhood. The *white light* would come when, for instance, at age four, she began singing in a nursery of napping children—she was told to keep quiet, which she could not. She must obey this light. Sometimes it drove her to sing, sometimes to pray. It was accompanied by an energy, which surrounded everything briefly, a rosebush, an orange, creating a nimbus and a shine for… maybe only a few seconds. Afterward, the world and she were changed. It was harder to describe *the fear*: it was horror of no one thing in particular, but a sense of a circle running all around her body isolating her totally from other humans giving a sense of terrifying responsibility and isolation to her being: it was a trembling that began without cause—like *the white light:* the fear of dislocation when one was about to leave one place and live in a new one. Being caught in limbo, no man's land: as if accompanied by an odd sense of perspective, a profound disorientation. She reached out for things and they shrank, or crumbled, pulverized, like powder, like mirages: the ground she walked on turned to water. It was this way the night she last walked on earth—after that, never again.

To lock hands with Lee even for ten seconds would have set the universe in joint.

Instead, after their feast, Lee set up a transfer chair in the narrow country bathroom. A rugged battle: a low wooden stool placed in the doorway afforded her something to transfer by from wheelchair, scraping the stool along the lino floor. *Life was not a level playing field.* Trying it out, she felt dizzy in the doorway.

Fatigue gnawed away at her, like a rat at bone. Through the grey film she'd rather spend this evening with Lee by the ocean than home alone. Occasionally, she felt as though she'd received a wing blow in the center of her chest, as though struck by a great bird. She felt it now, rigging up a blue night light in her room. Lee would sleep opposite down a long hall. After the suffocating wing blow, elbow-jab air would flood back into her lungs, which felt scraped. Long spaces between breaths came as though each were a step up a steep hill: her ribs felt held in iron.

Reaching her hand out to transfer she cut her index finger. She put it to her mouth, sucked the blood. Then bit her upper lip 'til it bled, tasting of metal. Lee, drawing back the covers on the cot, was unaware.

In these states, she often wished for a mate on the most practical counts. Her hands became shaky, lifting a teakettle equivalent to lifting a heavy rock. A shadow, a feather, could weigh like a stone. It might slip, her hand be scalded. All winter had only brought bitter argument upon argument with her mother who'd moved close to be of help but had ended up creating fresh trials, barging in with vacuum cleaner odd hours, rearranging pictures on the wall.

Watching Lee back at the stove, pouring tea, Sarne settled into the old green sagging couch. There were stacks of bookcases about this cottage, oil paintings of seascapes, piles of plants grey every which way on window ledges, an ancient radio played, an oil stove stood to the left center of the living room. There was a counter separating kitchen from living room so she could watch Lee clean up. Energy was type miracle, a slow burning candle that illumined the room.

Sarne is watching Lee. Doing things is the way Lee communicates her love, by acting. Lee was far more communicative of her love in the comparative silence of the dinner preparation than in the car ride down.

"Beginning to unwind?" Lee called out from the tap.

"Yes," Sarne closed her eyes. "Can I help you?" she called out.

"You've been packing. Rest up."

The dog was hungry. Lee set out his dish and the black lab fell to thumping his tail; nervous, eyeing them while here to see that they didn't leave him once more.

Looking into the kitchen, Sarne observed Lee, her fair coloring, natural blonde at almost forty. She'd prepared fruit salad for desert, removing the pip from each grape. She'd done this meticulously the way she'd pre-boiled the onions before putting them on skewers to broil.

Before putting the broils up in the fire-pit, before supper, Lee had slipped outside in her green-black mackinaw and desert boots. When she doused fuel on the flames, flames leapt up to illuminate her in relief against fire like the first human lighting a fire. Lovers always believe they are the first.

Sarne lit up two cigarettes after dinner. Lee was "agin' it." In addition to this, they had a low-keyed ongoing battle between the two: the Limeys ... had something gone wrong once between Lee and a person from Britain?

"They have such sharp distinctions between working class and upper class. The Limeys tend to see things too much in terms of money."

Lee was drinking, become more derogatory toward the Brits. Sarne could hardly hold her head up against the fatigue which now felt like waters, rising teeth high, inching their way into her very eyes.

"I'm going to get some sack, early," she said.

What a slat the bed was! Sarne had brought *The Bible*. If she placed a thick book under her coccyx it eased backache.

Lee was relaxed now. Crocked. Her face relaxed. She sat at the foot of the bed. Calm. Sculptural. Sarne wanted to kiss her.

But Lee left.

She would stir the pool of ashes in the fireplace at dawn, reheat the cooked potatoes. Lee would stay up half the night reading. The light from her bedside would throw a shaft down the hall, spilling under the lintel from the half-closed door.

Sarne could feel the boards of the house creaking, settling in. The dog, high-strung, barked a few times, then settled down. She could hear his breathing. Sarne was sleeping in the kid's bedroom. Peanuts cartoons hung about. She picked up an owl from the windowsill, lying flat on her back, reaching to the head of the bed. She'd been proofing stories and poems before leaving town, wanting things to be right, down to the last word. She closed her eyes to try sleep but kept seeing type. Words, printed, would flash across the backside of the stuffed giraffe, the zebra, and all those animals that stood in poses of action on the window-ledge.

She slipped into a light sleep, then woke and saw Lee's light had gone out. She could hear the heavy body settling into the double bed. Lee turned once or twice, then the easy deep rhythm of her breathing in sleep.

Sarne could feel the knife being twisted into her backbone. She'd thrown her dogtooth tweed car jacket over the foot of her cot. By two in the morning, she rose as quietly as she could, maneuvered the bathroom, took a pill for pain. She began floating...both arms spread. She could feel the wires in back of her neck loosen. The hawk. Both eyes peeled of lids. She saw everything. She saws two women leading their lives in the quiet country. Unfolding. As one unfolds impeccably clean sheets. She pictured their shared live in separate scenes. A homecoming.

"Lee," she whispered, "We'll go halves on the horse, yeh?"

"Ay," Lee whispered back. "On everything."

We'll refuse to let the soldiers pass us by in the marketplace."

"We'll refuse to drag about in petticoats."

"And if we must become hermits, so we will."

She was circling even higher now. So high it was scary. She wondered if she would ever descend again. Circling higher and higher above the cottage, she saw they were two palominos, with radiant eyes and beautiful manes, whispering to one another. She was so high now she could see more than Oregon, one third of the continental United States! California, Oregon, Washington appeared in tiny tracts under her eyes. She saw the two of them, high-strung, in the field. They were transposed back into human from horses; she saw them returning home to one another by evening, to make out of the ordinary acts of living an extraordinary thing: a consoling like that religion confers.

When she woke, it was to remember these words of Lee's, "Your body is not deformed, love, it is a beautiful one."

○

She heard Lee rise to go to the john. Night sloughed off. It became the eerie earliest beginning of dawn. She waited 'til she heard Lee turn the key in the ignition, to rise to a seaside shack alone in morning.

Lee had left reheated black coffee and some fruit salad from last night. She left the sink spattered with juice, plates from last night piled sloppily to the left of the sink.

"For the birds!" Sarne scoffed, flushing butts down the john.

She did transcendental meditation for twenty minutes every morning, then turned on the radio, got a Black music station, and then turned it off, drinking in silence. Stirred potatoes were in the cool ashes. She didn't want to remove the typewriter from the corner. She didn't want to hear its bell ring. "Chattererly, be silent," she chided, "Be not noisy like my mind."

She stared a long while out the window at fog billowing in waves from the sea, like steam cutting off cypress trees just at the knees, or leaving only tops in later morning.

Her hawk's eye perspective of the dream!

She'd soon extend her arc out into the Arizona desert. Lee said that when her own Ohio childhood faded, she'd remember that clay-red earth. Those stark contrasts of earth and sky would never fade.

She drew a cigarette out of her breast-pocket. Packed it down on the sink edge, didn't light up yet. Lay it on the table, neat nail. Slipped out another, another until there were six: laid them in a chain. She drew her shoulders back in the black turtleneck, no more blades of pain. Little boxcars going south, those trains she'd ridden with her younger sister, Alma, and her mother the winter she was nine, traveling east into Tampa, Florida, to get the divorce. The divorce, which sprang full-blown from the war like Athena from the head of Zeus. She'd met a Gentile girl that winter—she looked a bit like Lee, straight fair hair, wide gray eyes—with whom she'd sat bare-stocking on some pier overlooking the oily ash of water, the Gulf of Mexico. She'd taken the girl's hand, "Pray for me Bev, that my parents can join again? You've got the know-how, you're Catholic."

What Bev wouldn't have understood was her asking, please talk to God about it. "I don't know how to pray."

Sarne was being truthful in claiming she didn't know how to pray but she knew the white light and the fear, absolutely clear that they connected somehow, in some obscure way, with the act of prayer.

But they remained apart, Jo-Jo and Dr. Issacs, with the manner which seemed to calm the roiled sea whenever he entered a world of patients. Jo-Jo and her daughters remained poor; the baby had to travel home with the after-effects of a bad break at the hip. For, although Sarne was elfin, she hadn't the ability to intercede for miracles.

○

While Lee was teaching summer school, Sarne read through the house library in morning. She was chilled by two in the afternoon, Lee hadn't returned. Her hat and coat were ready for a drive back up coast to her mother's. When Lee did return, she poured them tumblers of red wine for a late lunch. Then she was to drive them up coast in nearly total silence, as though a curfew had been declared, or a gun cracked, past those Victoria gingerbread wooded houses in San Francisco, blue fog engulfing them.

"Don't expect mail, Kiddo, remember I'm not a letter writer," the words echoed in Sarne's ears. They stopped, to buy vegetables in a seaside shack, for a farewell party Lee was giving Sarne in two nights. During those five minutes Lee was gone from the car, Sarne cried. Fiercely, knifed over in the front car seat, her two sweater and dogtooth car coat on.

Then it was all over.

They returned to an apartment which was like a ghost town. Sarne's mother had removed the keys from the key-ring. Now only three more days countdown.

One thing Lee bought on her way home she opened in the car. A kiwi. It was evening once more, she handed Sarne the kiwi.

"Here, Kiddo," she said. "Bite it open."

"Not hungry," Sarne shook her head and looked out the window.

She lit a cigarette catching the orange butt reflected in the glass.

Lee didn't criticize this time.

A twinge of pain brought it back: Her mother, Jo-Jo.

Jo-Jo

Jo-Jo. Middle child, like Lee, but one whom her father adored. His dark-haired girl, who by her tenth year was competitive. Papa used to tease Jo-Jo that she was a good *boy*. She laughed, squaring back wide, oarsmen's shoulders, twisting lanky toes in the dust of their Texas backyard. Her Papa was a research chemist at a small college in west Texas, an odd place for a Jew to land. After training in the Old Land, Hungary, he brought his young, fine-boned Rumanian wife over to the New World in 1910, obtaining a research post at the Texas College, Brent. Jo-Jo's ma had an English and Romanian background, and although the girl was raised in West Texas, she always considered herself akin to the Yankees in her "rock bone" spirit. Her bosom pal from third grade on was a girl, Abigail, whose family had relocated from Massachusetts to Texas.

Jo-Jo was always a pariah: her right eye turned in. "Squint" they called it, politely. "Cross-eyed!" the kids on the playground taunted her.

She put her hands to her hips, stuck out her tongue, gave them the raspberries, and wound up mock-kicking them all, then turning and running.

"Jo-Jo, sweet," they came taunted.

"Go wash your feet—

The board of health's across the street."

Like her eldest daughter, Sarne, she was to find solace in the cool, impersonal eye of nature. The glance of God, she came to call it, deciding she'd always be an Ishmael. She wore the black patch 'til she was nine: then she was given glasses, but stomped on them in a vacant lot near her home and never wore them again. Her shoulders were wide-slung for a girl, and she was an exceedingly fast runner, like her athletic daughter.

Sarne's grandmother was a tiny, auburn-haired woman with two coppery braids wound round her head, in the old style. Her hands were quick at kneading dough, molding cookies. She'd been born a twin, but the boy got scalded by a vat of boiling water in the old Rumanian kitchen when they were still infant of three weeks. He died right away. Jo-Jo's mama, though petite, was a dynamo, who washed from morning 'til night in big tubs; gave birth to her first two children at home, the third—only because he was a breach birth—in the Texas hospital. She retained accents of Romania where she'd met her husband when he flew as a young man to Bucharest for a chemical conference. She rolled her r's strong even when she was in her seventies. People stopped her to tell her she had an English complexion, and resembled Queen Mary for which she'd thank them very kindly.

Jo-Jo's elder sister, Zaza, resembled a Hungarian Rosemary Clooney—the cheekbones! Blue-eyed, blonde, with only an occasional burst of temper. She wore black patent leathers pumps, bright lipstick, split-curls. She went to the prom, wore white gloves that stretched to the eye and carried a clutch purse while her kid sister, Jo-Jo, won the award for best all round camper the summer that they were eleven and nine.

Even by that time, Jo-Jo had developed her hand-eye coordination to the point where she could visualize a home-run—drawing upon instinct to know just how hard and high to whack the ball, how to run scraping into home, cutting all the other bases. She knew this, just the way her own daughter Sarne was born knowing there was a story her life would tell; would she become paralyzed? Yes, she must have known at some level, or else why those long rainy day rehearsals with Alma when they pulled down the curtain rods and strapped them on to "get the feeling" of being Emmy-Lou, the girl in third grade who'd had polio, had one withered leg on which she wore an iron brace? How could she have known? Yet she did. That her destiny was to become the March of Dimes poster child, now a boy, now a girl: androgynous. She came to know, Sarne did, that fate was simply what happened. She also knew by the age of eleven that life was a story, and the narrator should be like clear glass.

Her girl friends, like her mother's before her, had painted nails—some of them—and did all the things peculiar to growing up in the post-war forties in Sarne's case; in the roaring twenties, in Jo-Jo's—including going in giggling gangs to movies; dancing the Charleston 'til they drooped. Jo-Jo's friends became telephone operators and felt very proud of it. Sarne's sold records and books in the Berkeley bookstores, and those of other college towns, in the anti-war sixties. Jo-Jo's friends had names like Toots, Madge and Sissie while her younger brother, Jakela, wore sailor-suits.

Jakey was a Picasso type Saltimbanque, who physically resembled Jo-Jo a bit, but without her strong physique. It was more a resemblance of coloring: with his lustrous dark curls cut in the Buster Brown of the twenties. "Buster Brown" was stamped inside his saddle-oxfords, just as "Indian Walk' was stamped inside Sarne and Alma's shoes 'til Sarne could no longer walk, and Alma no longer wanted to dance. Sarne came down, in 1959, with what was called summer gripe during the Second World War in England. In the United States, it was called infantile paralysis.

Jake took to the sea. A Pisces, he swore that he could feel the pull of the ocean in his bones even dwelling in the desert dust. He wore his sailor-suit from the age of five 'til nine, when its blue-white sleeves faded, the lace was torn; his wrist cuff crawled clear up to his crusty elbows.

Then Jakela ran away from his strong maternal home to sea, at nineteen, joining the Navy, becoming part of the war with a Heart, 1943. A buccaneer at heart, he'd found his calling. Then the depression came and knocked the Charleston off its feet, and the black bottom came along. Zaza used to cut a mean rug: those were the days girls rolled back the carpet and danced 'til dawn with their sweethearts fresh home from the war. The era of Great Gatsby, the Flappers. Jo-Jo-s mother danced, still with her copper braids wound round her head in the manner of the Old World tucked away. Her performing daughter, when she grew older, attended the program from the Berengaria, where Jo-Jo had tap-danced to the delight of the sea captain of the Queen Mary II.

Jo-Jo held onto her gold ribbon "Best Girl-Athlete," and her green one, "Best All Around Camper," though she tucked them to the back of her socks and underwear drawer. She was one of Mary McCarthy's The Group, after all, later than the Flappers. An East coast intellectual, she'd chosen—of the three college scholarships she was awarded—to go ivy league, the full step into New England. She claimed it was in her blood, that rock bone Yankee, then entered the freshman class at Vassar in 1936.

She now only saw in scenes which floated before her eyes... the ballet dancer she'd dreamed of becoming 'til she found she had too muscular a body. But for two years, Jo-Jo had saved nickels for toe shoes, pink satin ones she'd seen in the window of that small Texas town where her daddy taught, and pointed out behind plate glass, sucking in her breath, with her mama. That was during the days of Victory stamps. In fact, she'd chosen the exact pair in the window of the Desert Ballet School. When her mother shook her head and said, "Jo-Jo, I'm afraid no," the girl had seen desert dust swirl up through her tears. A kind of dust devil of revenge.

Now she could stick her tongue out at no one. She knew the family was going through hard times.

But she dreamed toe shoes, slept, ate, and ran toe shoes that winter. Those satiny pink slippers went with her through hours of tedious mathematics, grammar, and spelling bees.

"Papa!" she pleaded.

'Your mama's right," he shook his head, "We've fallen upon hard times."

That didn't stop Jo-Jo. She tore wads of stuffed cotton out a burst sofa in the garage and stuffed them into the toes of her thick woolen knee socks: she stood on them in front of the bathroom mirror 'til her toes ached. 'til they turned black and blue, and started bleeding. She washed the blood out of her white socks in a panic. It was before her monthlies had started coming. Still, she danced hugging herself in the barn, humming the waltz under her breath, and sucking her lungs in.

Toe shoes wore off, or she finally gave up. But just about to enter her teens, Jo-Jo developed another infatuation; paint and easel. She'd passed The Old Masters Desert Studio a thousand times, going to the corner store, the nickel & dime, for milk, or Borax. That winter her appendix hurt; she had emergency surgery. Still sore from the appendectomy, she returned to Hungary for a visit with her parents. She was hauled along, through the art museum. All Jo-Jo could remember from that June was staring at the long-suffering faces of the Dutch Masters; Rembrandt's self-portraits looking as though his face were melting wax. Titus Son! Now, there was a boyo. She wanted to be—in fact, she saw herself as Titus' Son: rich copper-brown curls, like her mother, the kind she'd bequeath to her own child Sarne, who too became long-suffering.

They had no money for this, but took a side trip to Greece, with money borrowed from an uncle in Hungary. She gazed at Greek statues, at The Parthenon: With their noses chipped off, eroded features; with their arms fractured and jagged at shoulder joint or elbow they spoke to her of their pain, through her pain. Her body weighed a ton, was a bag of cement and bone to drag around. She felt like she weighed about two-hundred pounds that summer she was sweet sixteen. In realty, Jo-Jo was down to ninety-eight pounds.

"Pumping iron," that's me: she reminded herself, thinking of her anatomy text. Ninety percent water and pumping iron. She kept having to lie down in hotel rooms: in Greece, in Hungary. Dizzy, weak, she laid wet rags across her forehead to bring the sharpness back into her. Vision. Her vision, however, was always to return: or remain.

When her child, Sarne came to her one day and said, "A voice came to me from a cloud. I'm going to be a writer, Ma," she smiled recalling the voice from the cloud coming to her that summer she was sixteen. She simply nodded and Sarne knew she had a kindred spirit in her parent.

"I want to be a painter, Mama," she begged now. "Let me stay on in Greece."

"Weak as you are, you entertain that idea?" her mother said.

"I'm getting strong. France, the Louvre."

But again they said no and brought a reluctant Jo-Jo home.

She dreamed all that winter about the golden opportunity she'd passed by: studying at the Louvre.

"Who guarantees you'd be accepted by an art school in Paris, no less, Jo-Jo," her mother tried to bring her back to earth.

"And in the northern light! In winter. The most scrutinizing light in the most scrutinizing season."

It was because she was a rock bone Yankee deep down and they didn't understand her all that this had been denied her, and she'd been forced to return to the west Texas town.

"It's not the worst place on earth, Jo-Jo," her mother smiled, over hot tea and muffins.

"This town feels very old, mama, old and sad. Yet it's got no history, no burnish in the least."

Jo-Jo set her chin to her palms, elbows on table, and simply stared her mother down.

Later, to her daughter Sarne, she said, "If you really want to learn about my era, read about the dance marathons. See *They Shoot Horses, Don't They?* They were fast!" Jo-Jo told Sarne.

She could beat out the boys at gym races, 'til most of the boys wouldn't taker her on. What could she do with athletics she thought? Her English teacher had eyeballed her, in the final year of high school; she could be a crack good writer if she tried. But she decided if she should get lucky, and win one of three scholarships to the good women's college in the East, she'd turn them all down and spring for the Arts Students League in New York City and take an apartment in Greenwich Village with a girlfriend. When she'd decided to go to art school, her father put his foot down, and said no.

So she did enroll at Vassar, where, after being advised to take a heavy dose of liberal arts, Jo-Jo went and signed up for six hours of Physical Chemistry just to flaunt her father. It was her first term.

She was bound to fail and did.

It was slow suicide.

She was put on probation.

In high, she'd scraped by—getting splinter in her palm—getting C's in math and chemistry. She began Vassar with ten hours a week in labs, bending over Bunsens.

Six failed hours meant automatic probation.

Having begun on the wrong leg, Jo-Jo figured she'd no where to go but downhill. And fast! This despite the fact she earned flying A's in Greek. Prodigal daughter. Dirty hope. "And," her father's voice came after her, "you were my boy, my son."

She shaved off her hair. Not in the bob of the twenties, but really shaved, like a young woman Buddhist monk, like a shorn lamb.

Looking like a youth on the head of a Greek coin, she packed up her one ball gown, two cardigans, easel, a few aborted canvases, a half dozen unfinished stories, and left Vassar to set up on her own in New York City's Greenwich Village.

Those were the days of theatre. The Provincetown Players—whom she joined for a while, but was told her voice wasn't strong enough to project in the legitimate theatre, and she knew no way to break into the silver screen.

There was dance. Jo-Jo enrolled in some of Martha Graham's early experimental classes in modern dance. She leapt the way Isadora Duncan leapt. She wept with Dietrich. With a flair for whatever she did, she took up paint and brush, painting some dramatic oil paintings with vibrant, autumn colors like her birth. She painted flowers which were volatile: a combination of her panache, and her inherited sharp, critical eye. In the Village, she met a handsome Jewish psychologist with whom she fell in love: both mirror and contrast to her father: reflective of her father's brilliant mind, but with a wild, almost arrogant, gypsy streak of his own.

She married him—who had once thought she'd marry no one. But was she ever truly happy? Did the repression at her father's hands come out in words to her older daughter? "You may come to my funeral," she smiled to Sarne at lunch, "and sit in the front row where you may see all the flowers that have been brought in."

She read books about how early women painters in the Connecticut valley had improvised paints out of berries and brickbats. "They sold their paintings for 23 cents to neighbors, or they'd bartered them to gypsies," she told Sarne. "Look hard at what your father has left me! Filthy lucre! Filthy lucre!"

She tore up the child support check of fifty dollars one month in front of her two daughters.

The dark handsome Jew, who resembled her father in some ways, had—like her father—let her down. He was married to his work, not to Jo-Jo. Once more, love had passed her by.

A headstrong girl before marriage, had she ever cleaned house before?

Was marriage to force her to pass the whirlpool at Hell's Gate?

But she loved her children. And even after her marriage, Jo-Jo had yearned to paint. Her children saw her possessed by a force, perhaps a demon? Even greater than her maternal love for them. She set up one of her huge canvases on the living room easel after Sarne's polio and painted clear through suppertime.

Had Jo-Jo simply waited out her time? 'Til her girls were teens, her husband driven? Like that central hush, that blur in the eyes, with which the quail waited? Was inspiration still hers, or lost to her? No. She could grasp it still! Free time came again, free of threat, when she might venture to cross the road again. To leave the girls half an hour in the evening to buy cigarettes at the corner—sharing some with Sarne willingly. "Why not? Life's dealt you a raw blow, kid!" she'd say—her language reminiscent of the later Lee.

It was all right now to paint 'til one or two in the morning. To take a lover? But she wanted none. Bed had been her martyrdom.

"Never expect your happiness in life, girls, from men," she'd announced bitterly one day.

What Jo-Jo didn't tell her daughters was that she'd close her eyes, bite her tongue—sometimes drawing blood—'til the lovemaking was all over. She resented his opening bills before kissing her on returning home in evening. But after all, he'd been a poor boy. She resented the way he'd pore over his lecture-notes and medical articles in the evening rather than listening to Caruso with her. After all, he'd loved his Caruso records and brought them all, his form of dowry into the marriage. The living room grew large and increasingly lonesome in the evenings, "And you realize, your father, Sarne and Alma, insisted that you girls be out of sight, put to bed, tucked in by seven each evening—even though he continued his own reading and shared with me little, nothing. She dreaded their social outings. The beautiful and happy wife of Dr. Issacs, she'd be brought to dances for inmates of the mental institutions. She began to feel like an inmate herself. She resented his Yiddish from Brownsville, thrown into his words of affection, his rarely voiced feelings. She minded his seedy, frayed jacket elbows, the hiked shoulders of the youth intent upon his books reading, walling the rest of the world out. Jo-Jo began to make fun of his friends.

She deplored his trying out the Rorschach on her, those early days of psychologist tests while the war was still raging. Sarne remembered the two of them, her parents when they were married, bent over the dining room table, in a light so forlorn, yellow, dangling by a chain from the ceiling, the two of them sat, looking like figures Rockwell Kent had drawn with his charcoals, a severe medium. It was one of the few times she saw them as a couple. Jo-Jo was supposed to be interpreting inkblots, her father writing it all down.

"But more, give me more, Jo-Jo. Everything."

How could she give him everything when he gave her nothing?

And her child—she felt the presence of the shadow in the lamplight—hovering.

They lived outside the Army post. Jo-Jo made no friends. She had inherited, after all, her own father's critical turn of mind toward people, books, art—everything. She could look upon them as Daumier satires, caricatures rather than as individual, suffering humans. Or Sarne's father, Aaron Isaacs, saw it this way. Perhaps, in reality, Jo-Jo never failed to discern the suffering: the real from the superficial, the shallow, the self-seeking which she found evident among psychologists and physicians. By the time the marriage dissolved, Sarne's father said he had no friend left she hadn't made a joke about, and made even him see the ridiculous side of. The devil of it was that she was always right in some particular. Though exaggerated, her comments held some core of truth. She latched onto this for the butt of a joke which turned cruel.

But the births of her two daughters, particularly the first one, were transcendent occasions for Jo-Jo who sang all night, the nurses told her, the night Sarne was born.

Jo-Jo once told Sarne she had, in fact, begun to be sad with her husband on their honeymoon when he guilted her for buying a bottle of hand lotion. Once, during the war, when Aaron returned on surprise twenty-four hour leave, she nearly didn't let him in.

"You could be a fine painter," the Russian sculptor. Alexander Archipenko, had told her during her brief studies with him.

"But you think of yourself as a woman."

Still she began sculpting when Sarne was two years old: heads of this child.

This child magnetized, haunted her, a thing Sarne felt with both exalting and fearful sometimes. Her child was fair, like the grandmother. The girl was closer in spirit to her grandmother than to anyone else in the family.

"*Kakuzala*" her Russian paternal grandmother called her.

Like Jo-Jo, Sarne had been born with a squint which showed up at age five: but Sarne's was in the left eye, one of the several physical eccentricities to mark her existence. Jo-Jo spent hours, patient as a saint, particularly considering her temperament, with orthotics: every night toward the end of the war. Together, they moved the wood and glass device back and forth on the stick, 'til they caused the boy in knickers to leap through the brown-wood hoop.

Slowly both eyes fused to make one in sight.

Sometimes, Sarne would lie and say the boy had jumped through just to get free of the task.

Jo-Jo was able to divert her disappointment over marriage into the rearing and ripening child, pouring all her energies into her. Then, through the later, more docile child, Alma. She didn't want Sarne to be an only child, but she made it clear to Sarne that even when she conceived Alma she'd made up her mind, fast and firm, upon divorce.

The vision! The vision had again kicked in that she'd have to be free of Aaron Issacs one day in order to earn anything near happiness, even contentment, back again. But she waited 'til her own father, suffering a series of early strokes, died, for he had been against the marriage from the word go. She stiffened her backbone, Jo-Jo, to the letdown of her own marriage, a woman with a will hard as saddle-leather.

"Nothing can break your integrity!" her husband had hurled at her. She never would take his counsel, "Act defenseless, Jo, and then you'll get people to give you some help."

So she'd kept up the front of a peaceful, even a happy, marriage all those years.

A decade of delusion.

Then, after V day, she discovered Florida was a state where adultery needn't be the sole cause of divorce in 1947, like in New York. So she took a train trick for the tree of them to ride into the South. She traveled two days and three nights into the South, her two young girl-children at either side like baskets. She'd a knack for making home wherever they were—she cultivated this during the war. With a flourish, she'd light a match to an oil stove. She'd set out a daguerreotype—her mother, her grandmother. And she had the finest pair of shoulders Sarne had ever seen on a woman. So there, of all places in Tampa, Florida, after nine months of waiting the divorce came through.

"Look, girls!" Jo-Jo held up the white piece of paper one morning in early spring. "The Freedom Papers."

But prior to that, it had been a rotten, a challenging, a testing winter. Alma had fallen between twin beds playing with Sarne and broke her leg at the hip, a nasty break. Bone shattered. It was Christmas Eve. The girls had been horsing around. Jo-Jo always held Sarne to blame for this.

"Will God forgive me? Pray God to forgive me?" the lanky nine-year-old, shivering, wept into a neighbor woman's arms to whom she was farmed out for the night while the surgeon drove in from outside Tampa to set the bone. And he was not sober.

My luck, Jo-Jo decided. I've been born under an evil star. After all, Jakela once said so.

The bone took four months to mend. When the cast was removed, Alma's leg appeared purple and yellow, blotched. Worse than both Sarne's legs after polio. But the limb hadn't been exposed to air. Jo-Jo saw to it that it would be now. She carried the four year old on her shoulder, along the beach, to let the sun get at the bad leg 'til the blood flowed freely again and the child learned to walk without a limp, the picture of health by winter's end.

Though Jo-Jo had cried out to Sarne, in her anguish Christmas Eve, as she left in the ambulance for the hospital with Alma and the doctor, "Ask God to forgive you." Sarne had taken it literally and prayed, "Dear Lord, forgive me for fracturing Alma's leg," though Sarne knew in her heart of hearts it was her mother that must forgive her. Sarne drove her fist into the pillow at the neighbor's that horrifying night. She adored her baby sister more than anyone in the world.

But what was that to Sarne contracting polio at age twelve?

It was 1951: summer had just begun. A shimmering time. Vacant. No plans. It was an odd time, outside-time. For the first year in three, the girls weren't going to summer camp high in the Catskills like the previous two summers, when Sarne had a love affair with the ease with which her body obeyed her commands: to swim, to sleep in lentos, to tan and grow like berries in the sun. Sarne was on the cusp of childhood adolescence. School had only been out a few days, she'd made one downtown trip on the bus for a dime, to New Rochelle's leafy elm-shaded, early century inner core, to browse Kresske's with her best friend, Sammi-Sue. They'd bought their first Tangee lipstick, and tried it on in the drugstore mirror—orange popsicle color. Camisoles, midriffs, of peppermint green and Dutch blue. Sarne felt an overwhelming hollowness in her chest, coming down New Rochelle's Main Street right after they bought the Tangee. The plate-glass windows with their nude mannequins looked left over from some war. Sad, they needed a spiffing up, certainly a dusting. The First Trinity Church looked flat as a brick church really made of cardboard for a movie set. The feeling created a throwback to the dirty thirties, the forties when she came into being. There was an odd, metallic taste to this summer before it had begun, like blood on the tongue. She lay on her back in bed at night and cupped her hands over the small breasts like round firm oranges she could feel forming beneath her undershirt: perfected, they might be like two miniature St. Paul's domes in London, by Christopher Wren.

Home, she put one of her two pop records on, *I'll Never Let You Go Why Because I Love You.*

"You'll never let me go because you love me ..."

There was that empty, hollow, floating feeling again. *The fear.* She'd have spoken to God about it if she'd been able perhaps like that southern Catholic girl child so long ago. Instead, she poured herself a cream soda, stirring with a straw, grabbed a dusty blue and a dead yellow library book off the kitchen table.

For some reason, she'd taken out biographies, books stiff with facts, different books this summer from earlier: not the usual novels and romances. She'd made herself read every word of black print on white page of *My Polio Past.* It wasn't an interesting book. It was dry, told without emotion, despite the devastating ground, which it covered. Not a soul on earth had recommended it to her. No one had given a book report on it in school. It was a dreary medical account of treatment after treatment all of which failed in the long run, all a great trial, but a washout. The dreary book had a dirty yellow cover. She'd lain on her stomach, feet sagging about in the breeze, or still warm air of early July, chin propped on elbows, as she loved. She'd forced herself to take the whole canvas in but was glad when she could close the cover. Another book she'd taken out which—in retrospect seemed prophecy, was titled *No Time for Tears,* this about a young boy who suffers some accident or illness and is instilled with stoic philosophy which ran the world post-war: stiff upper lip, no time to cry.

Alma woke up with a stiff neck one morning. "Mother, should we call the doctor? Alma could have Polio!" Sarne was terrified. But Alma aborted whatever she had. Alma's was a false alarm.

She was the one who woke in the middle of the next night the knife twisting in her backbone, unable to pass water, knifed over in her mother's bed the sheet wringing, her pink summer nightie soaked clear through.

It was a wild crazy nightmare: she had gone to sleep aching, but woke past midnight feeling glass was breaking inside her legs and neck and spinal column; she climbed the five stairs from her loft-bedroom in that castle-type house in the suburbs down to Jo-Jo's room, whom she wakened, screaming. Banging the windows down, Jo-Jo didn't want the neighbors to be wakened.

"I can't pee," Sarne cried, sitting on the toilet time after time, unable to release her bladder. It was becoming paralyzed. Jo-Jo wouldn't phone the pediatrician 'til dawn.

The night lasting forever 'til dawn, then Jo-Jo phoning the doctor who came by in morning, then again in evening and ordered the ambulance.

The last thing Sarne did, when her legs could hardly lift they were so heavy was—although forbidden—to go to the doorway where a horrified, mute Alma stood and give her a kiss.

The ride into the little country hospital passed a greenhouse in the poorer part of town. In the blazing heat, the knife-like pain of paralysis coming on, Sarne registered everything neither in the white light or the fear, but with heightened light as though all were a hallucination, or else seen through a jolt of electricity shot through the veins.

"We're going to give you a spinal tap," the nurse said. "Turn on your side like an unborn baby."

They thrust the needle into her spine, while Sarne curled up in the fetal position. Then, Sarne rolled back onto her back, knees drawn up, hiking down her old pink nightgown down over her boyish hips.

"You're the first child we've ever given the spinal tap who didn't cry," the nurse told her.

"Why cry?"

Sarne looked out at New Rochelle dusk, the trees dusty, tired and old as sun set that endless day which had finally broken to follow that night which never would end.

Jo-Jo waited outside the tiny lab where the pediatrician slipped the slide under the microscope.

"My first polio!" she heard him exclaim.

Aaron drove out immediately, looking gaunt, ashen, with a doctor cousin to drive with Sarne into New York City where the hospitals had iron lungs. The previous summer had been an epidemic one, an overflow of polios crowding into hallways. Lungs were left. They traveled with the doctor-cousin so that if it got to Sarne's lung fast, a tracheotomy could be performed in the ambulance.

As she was being wheeled off the elevator toward isolation she remembered the trance-like calm she felt, the ecstasy, looking upon her father's face like a saint: he could heal anything. People relaxed around him, put their trust in him.

As soon as her father, Aaron Issacs, came Sarne felt she was in God's hands. Dr. Aaron Issacs had a brilliance in his agility combined with gentleness: his hands were long and supple, his voice was quiet but firm, she let herself be drawn into the relaxed state of one totally at anther's loving command.

In isolation, she turned to the nurse:

"What's wrong with me? Will I die?" she asked the nurse.

"You'll know in time."

Sarne thought she had spinal cancer."

She was fed through a tube in her arm. She was catheterized. The fourth of July came in a blaze of blue: one square of sky she could glimpse from her white bed the linen becoming wringing often, so changed.

A few New York city smokestacks were visible on the horizon in those soft muted colors of old brick, torn rose, terra-cotta, browns only New York, tired old giant of a city in summer time especially when dust-mites float in the air from the exhausts of a long summer's day, like pulverized sculptured stone.

"Don't you wish I'd die?" she asked the nurse whose face she couldn't see.

"No," the nurse said in a flat voice.

"What's wrong with me?"

"You'll know soon."

◯

So this was the script that was to unroll before them that summer when nobody knew what to do, knew perhaps instinctively better than to make any plans; that July which kicked off the decade of the fifties: this was the scenario mapped out for the three of them, the quarter acre of hell they were able to turn into a haven. The three graces, Jo-Jo, Sarne and Alma.

"It's not fair," she remembered telling that Gentile girl down south, years ago during the divorce, "Pray for me my parents get together again!" She didn't want to say because *you have the ticket*, that winter when Southland overwhelmed them. But she knew there was no point in saying, "So talk to God about it."

Her father who could calm the roiled waters had placed a bedside angel to her right. The nurse flicked the bedside radio on. The first song she heard just before being taken out of isolation was "*C'mon a my house, my housa c'mon,*" sung by Rosemary Clooney in her rusty, throaty voice.

Sarne asked for a Coke while the radio crooner crooned. Sugar.

"Can I have some *jujubes* and a Coke?" she asked.

She drank it through a bent straw, glass, a hospital straw. Coke never tasted better.

Then they lifted her onto a wooden board eight feet long, laid her on the scale on the floor. She'd never been that far from the ceiling. She looked up. It was like looking at the Sistine! She could see little maps and angels flying. She was shivering. Wearing only pad and gown, she was being weighed. She'd been close once to the ceiling of the huge gymnasium, close enough to horrify her—once, rope-climbing.

"Fifty-one pounds."

"Can I have a mirror?"

She wanted to look at herself. She didn't look much in the mirror but it had been seven days since she'd even consulted the old crooked bathroom one.

She looked different. But her eyes were green, brighter green, as if she'd been through fever and rinsed. She set the hand mirror face down on the bed, and then she reached her hands up to feel if they were still there. Yes, there under her hospital gown were the two firm young oranges, like perfectly rounded domes of St. Paul's by Christopher Wren.

○

A chapter in the book of her life was closed. She was wheeled on a plinth down the hall to a room of four children. She still didn't know what she had. But then, she'd only seen her parents through isolation, the round glass in the door of her room. She'd had no chance to talk with them.

She heard a child screaming and asked why.

"Because he has polio."

"I'm glad I didn't have that," said Sarne.

"You did."

She stared out the window in her new room. Now she understood that it wasn't something strange, dark, and unwritten about; something not to be read up on or seen on any posters anywhere, buried: cancer of the spine. She had suffered something that would connect her up with other people, with other children who'd been taken prisoner.

When Aaron and Jo-Jo Issacs came for their visit that afternoon, their pale tall daughter, looking very Egyptian, the nurse afterward told her, stretched out under fresh sheets, knees slightly bent, said, "You don't have to worry about telling me what I had. I know it was polio."

Had they not wanted to tell her not to scare her? When it was acute? Not to have her believe she'd be paralyzed for life?

"It means I'll never walk again, right? Like Samantha-Sue."

"Sammy-Sue may have had a more severe case."

"No. I suspect it was less severe. She had only one leg involved. I can't move either."

Jo-Jo and Aaron turned white as sheep, looked down to their shoes, and then looked their twelve-year-old child in the eyes as Aaron had always taught his daughters to give the truth their gaze.

Now came the months of pressing the wheel, the cross par, the splint, and prop—all those mechanical aids, those geometric shapes like chain hoists for bathtubs, the bone stays for corsets—all those devices to put the world in place again, to create movement without the use of limbs.

Sarne would lie in bed counting spokes to the wheelchair wheel; marveling at the many bolts and parts to simply one brace, then stare down at her right leg and think—how complicated the device, how simple, how God-like simple, the limb.

Still, she was super-excited at the prospect of getting out of bed, or moving again.

After isolation came the transfer to State Rehabilitation Hospital, where the state paid so much a day for your bed. Here, baths were like being weighed on the floor: under high windows, with grey winter light bathing the atrophying limbs, a child was lifted by a medieval type device called the Homer Heist, into a vat type tub, like that out of the Marat de Sade, and bathed by the hands of nurses who were not gentle. And just coming into puberty. This was the essence of being made voiceless, a victim.

Not so the ward, the ward of the children, the ward gang, developing their own language. By then they were becoming toughened. Some of the older teens even taught the pre-teens how to light up in the hospital bathroom—there were two for each ward. This is where Sarne learned.

Tilting her head at a rakish angle, she fancied herself a blonde Audrey Hepburn, gamine, member of a street gang of the mildest kind.

The hospital was like an old monastery, the ward one long room with high vaulted ceiling and beds on either side. The season was summer into autumn into winter. By winter, silver nitrate had been swabbed into the wound. Every tone on the gamut of pain had been wrung, from steaming hot backs where children were flung face down over wine barrels—that big—to bend the spines again. Tilt-tables, where the paralyzed body was strapped into belts and slowly the plinth-like table was tilted, a few more degrees each day, until the child stood in standing position. The blood returning to paralyzed limbs made circles of purple and orange. The autumn colors broke like shards of stained glass. The narration of my life, the story, must be like clear glass, Sarne thought once again.

So this was what had become of the summer of 1951: transformation. The child Sarne was transformed into Sarne the adolescent, on the brink of puberty, suddenly turned from her slim to super-thin, her fair complexion now almost translucent with that hectic flush in the cheeks of a child who has been gravely ill. Grave illness brings about a chemical change: thinned, she was also sharpened. She was visionary now seeing tales and sermons in everything. The world had come alive for her. Doing less, she heard more, saw more from a fixed vantage point.

Summer was never to be mellow, benign from that time on. It was to be a pitilessly, mercilessly lucid, revealing the very pits in the stone like those that became visible to Sarne those moments before and after the spinal tap that early July evening, that eternal evening. Summer was without mercy, but with much meaning. Mystical at times, mesmerizing.

When the rattan wood chair appeared as though by sleight-of-hand at the side of her bed in late autumn, before the final leaves had loosened their hold, she was amazed at how quickly she'd turned from a walking child into one who'd use a wheelchair from now on. It wasn't long before she was wheeled, still on plinth, to the German brace maker's shop in the basement of the rehab institution. Here it was! The shiny freezing steel she'd loved and hated; been magnetized to touch on the child who'd had polio and who wore the old-fashioned high boot with leather laces. Sarne had wanted to be in class with her, simply to help lace the high shoe and strap the leather thongs of the brace around the purple withered leg.

She returned home with her new braces and crutches.

The next seven years were the toughest, the most grueling in a life which by now did seem to hover under an evil star. Sarne and her mother, in the long, futile battle for Sarne to regain her legs, felt like star-crossed lovers, Romeo and Juliet.

There was no iron lung. There was no striker frame. There was no spinal fusion.

But there were years and years of physiotherapy at home, with old therapists from Jewish Berlin. There was the first winter, learning crutch-walking with long leg braces and steel boned corset, then curb climbing in New York City. There were wardrobes which never would fit 'til Jo-Jo began sewing her own outfits for her child. And all this after six months incarceration in a concentration camp for children—,where Alma was only allowed one visit through a window, tears streaming down the faces of both daughters, mirror-images now of each other in the winter of their lives.

Once, lifting the heavy collapsible wheelchair in one of the several jeeps Jo-Jo bought them she cried to Sarne, "We are star-crossed you, and I. Doomed."

There was the necessity every summer of going some place where there was swimming: a lake, a pool. Because one was without gravity in the water; Sarne could become a water child again!

And of course, she did it all alone.

In her mounting frustration, she was alternately kind—endlessly imaginative, turning the round bedroom into a castle, setting up desk with pads of papers and pens—and harsh with her daughter, at energy's end, wit's end.

During Sarne's hospitalization, Jo-Jo came every weekend to sit beside her daughter' bed. She made the world to follow polio seem a treasure-trove stored with gold: she brought in detailed street maps of Paris.

"We'll go there one day, you and I."

"And Alma?"

"Alma too. Of course."

She brought writing pads. And these, got scribbled on at night after the master switch was thrown and the children's ward all but darkened. She didn't know about the terrible limb-stretching, however; the searing burn of Sister Kenny Hot packs: steaming wool, which stank of urine, laid on each affected limb for an hour at a time.

Jo-Jo had failed at everything she undertook in life: ballet, art, her marriage, now this daughter, and her golden girl, stricken. But here, she would succeed. For the vision was now gnawing away: deep into her bone. The bone of her spirit was afflicted this time.

Little did she know—or did she know? In the room down the railway hall on Manhattan's Upper West Side, her daughter, in the small bedroom she shared with Alma, too, was experiencing the vision? The white light alternated now with the fear she'd known as a child. Only now, paralyzed, the white light won! In the dark, as snow whirled in a gentle cone of light on West Seventy Fifth Street, Sarne was brooding over the egg; incubating her first poems.

"There's no telling where this might end," Jo-Jo came in, smiled, put her arm around her daughter propped up in bed on one elbow, writing.

Child Revealed

Like a child unfurled from a flower, all of a sudden, a crocus from the blue bath child comes Belle, come I.

We find comfort—the beatitudes and brutalism behind all our grander

Aspirations and fictions. Like a prairie coming out of winter, I feel ice cracking, heart armoring breaking, and these days while Sweetheart finds a bruise spot on the zucchini. After hiding, comes disclosure. The violation. Whether rape or verbal abuse, at the hands of priest, teacher, or in my case at the hands of doctors.

The child's body is stripped, naked as a willow wand, and scrutinized under strobe lights. Conference time in the big state institution which used to house wounded military. A Civil War pavilion could not be starker.

Of course, the performer too lays his heart bare. My sister steps out upon stage and her heart is opened to everything.

I am high as a kite this morning on truth telling. One skips, the rope flies over the head, then thwacks the ground.

At first, I was a little saint? None of it because then the young demon underneath. Wet but not unwashed, nor was I among the great unwashed. Raw footage still exists. Ghost planes and outsourcing terrors are terms used in today's news. Coal companies, nonetheless, are still very much in the picture. Sit under rain, you get wet.

All life is a collage. I have just priced re-covering an old barrel chair. It's over the top. No way to beat out the competition.

Why are christening dresses so huge? To honor God? It's enough puff and lace to cover anything. They are a dizzying, cream-white four times the size of babies. Like the Reese jackets we wore. Our grief, of course, swallowed us. The christening dresses are somehow macabre.

Pinholes in wax paper let air in so angel fireflies can take oxygen.

Sweetheart sasses me about a garter belt. She cannot be serious. All three children in her family have married people who are their elders. Does that mean that their mother was absent from the nursery?

Let me ask you a question.

How does a prairie prepare for winter? We trim the lamps, we lay in fuel, we safety-check storm windows. We make the gray crystalline. We are not in Holland. We are in Canada where few windmills turn even across the flatland prairies. Canada is a country where there is the lore and love of old silos and grain elevators. An entire romance has developed around them.

I am the land, the prairie, I hoard wartime, I seal over with frost. I am a quilt gently covering eternal rest.

○

Today, I handed the woman at Ivy 's Place Books my new book.

"You just crank them out."

How does one write? One opens a vein.

Stores. I get my stories from them. There is the transgendered art dealer who's said, "All the years in the dark. I was in the back, in the shadows, framing. Now life is beautiful I wanted to be a ballerina," she twirls in a purple pants suit. I knew I was a girl ever since I was a little boy. Now, with the change I may go into clothing."

I hug her.

"Welcome to beyond the fringe."

"If you're not living at the fringe, you're taking up too much space."

Last week, our florist bought a twenty-two pound turkey and wanted to cook it on the rotisserie. It was too heavy for the rotisserie to turn so her son brought over his screwdriver. It basted while they gardened, raking last autumn leaves out back. When they came back gravy has spattered over the walls but the turkey was perfectly done.

Children in the ward, we felt the first frost come on. I closed my eyes and a combination of ammonia and blue light make evening. Is it more terrible to think people accidentally kill their children—say, by an overdose of sedatives if they are doctors, then cover the traces—than to imagine this time? Like the frozen Thames that winter when stores were built upon the river ice, this time is sealed over but was solvent underneath, seeming whole heart whereas in reality, like Pieter Breughel the Elder evoked cold on canvas, it was illusory. This was gray. There was no crystalline.

I don't dare carry glass.

The winter after the ballet academy, martial arts reigned. There was the fire. Then the ice. Ghost-strengths danced, *pas de deux*. Hands overheads. No bombastic paeans of praise of appeals for mercy, unhidden child, you were forbidden life's wild feast still.

A life in the arts comes full circles for her parents, for my cellist and her black dancer born in Harlem, having given thirty-seven years to the innovative dance, studying with Martha Graham.

Alabama Light & Power Co

Sundays are too thin for me: fit like a straight jacket or a marriage sheathes not the bouffant baby's christening gown.

O

I was not a fairy tale princess come back in the wrong skin. Our clothes hung in a tin closet on flimsy hangers beside our hospital cots. Is this the reason I keep making it up to myself? I have bought Sweetheart a waffle weave cream pullover with brown leather buttons obliquely swathed address the neck for her birthday, her sixtieth-- how can that be?

Delicate, iridescent, the Thames froze over. Unflinching, the boys haunted us in our reveries while we painted miniatures of love with perspective on home from the ward. In its history, the heart ices several times, perhaps one dozen. Oh the oxen. We are Christless, but Christened. In its long history, the river Thames has frozen solid forty times. Each time has a different circumstance, collection of memories of the river. Vignettes between 1142 and 1895. Achingly beautiful, a photograph etching scenes in our imagination. Queen Matilda tried to escape her besieged castle in a snowstorm, lover met on the frozen water in plague years, a farmer persuaded his oxen ice was safe, moments fleeting transformative for watcher and actor, for beholder and held. Pennants flew; there was a diffusion of snow crystals. The apple crier is frozen, her mouth in an "o." Some winters were so cold that birds froze to death, symbols of spring. People of England took birds into their houses 'til spring returned. In some girl's rooms were two robins, building a nest on roof beams over fireplace flittering all day gathering hair and bits of straw to stow in nests. The mother takes broom to them when they fly over her cook stove. The father worked the rail yards and comes home with stories of rabbits eating oil from trains. The robins brought home in his coat pocket sometimes swipe down for pieces of cheese, an apple rind, the sister's tea towel not beating them back. They bathe in the basin water at the far end of the girl's bed. I think of all this in the hospital.

1951 was my year.

1895 was the winter of the twelve-week frost. From December end the mid March all England was plunged into bitter cold like ladle in a pot. The Thames was totally blocked by enormous ice floes for a week in February. Horse drawn coaches crossed the Thames at Oxford where on the Kingston ice a carnival was set underway, capped with roasting an ox ceremonially. Ships wee frozen into mooring; lightermen weren't able to land to off-load cargo. The Grand Surrey Canal between Botherite and Old Kent Road featured crews of men dispatched to break ice in order for coal supplies to pass on their accustomed river route. But the ice the men broke, throwing it onto the banks, formed an enormous ice wall for protection, ten feet high, two miles long.

That winter had little snow. A pond in Yorkshire froze all the way to the bottom, like an elevator in its shaft. An anachronism. We took the ritual, or at least I did, of two hours chafing, one hour for each leg from toes to thigh, to get warm enough to sleep, things smooth as a hard-boiled egg, satin, an oyster. It grew warm enough for snow. *Flocons de neige*[1]. Gray or stairwells, wards, tubs were shot through with crystalline. That whole winter was a long meditation on the nature of frost and cold.

Although suddenly the sun!

Suddenly it would shine, liquid gold, amber. Last night I had an orgasm and this morning I want to wear red stockings! O beatitude and brutalism we laid them all bare. There are books *Frostiana* and *Frost Fairs on the River Thames*. But who has documented our year? Only the imagination italicizes it with a stiletto of sterling silver, a nib that cuts it all in, yet in relief like black ink, like frozen bodies or houses a lamp glows inside, which eerily turns to marble the gray which was crystalline.

---

1   *Flocons de neige* means snow flakes.

Plenteous Redemption: A Trilogy of Stories

"With the Lord there is steadfast love, and with him is plenteous redemption."
        Psalm 130:7

"Whenever you are fed up with life, start writing: ink is the great cure for all human ills."
        C.S. Lewis to his Arthur Greeves, 1916

Not Rain—Liquid Sunshine: Plenteous Redemption

"Sing! You two, driving home from the funeral—just as you always used to."

Forgive me for shining this one up and putting it in front of you. Our salad days had come. Yet still there was a quality of starvation which haunted our world. I am twelve, in the hospital after polio, which has paralyzed me from the waist down. Theatre curtains above morphed into coarse, cheap linen hospital curtains hung on plumbing piping and, like a shower curtain, pulled by its metallic cord and metal circles to match. The curtains shabby and old but once rich velvet: this is setting the scene for my entire life. A camera on the side catches us. We are transparent, that close to breaking, not wood. My dirty blond braid is coming loose in Silentville, half way to my fanny. We have been transplanted, we three transparencies.

We arrived in the country, where the cabins are in the wake of a tragedy—the loss of three young men in a horrific traffic accident, during rush hour to the ferry. A fully-loaded dump truck collided with their car and nine others, setting the three young men on fire. One was the best friend of Erin-Eileen's twenty-year-old grandson.

Redemption seemed more and more thin, whipcord thin—further and further away, an unreachable branch, an oasis in the desert till, like an angel, it could dance on the head of a pin.

Once again, my Yorkshire friend had to rise to heroic heights, leading her family through the grieving. Her grandson became pallbearer, whose closest schoolfellow and playmate had caught fire and died.

Summertime always lays me flat anyway, it being the time my legs were taken away.

It was the first for this getaway cabin in twenty acres of forest on the ocean.

We had come to the country for a week. There were architectural barriers I could see from the car even before I got out. It was not level, there was one step on a block of concrete in front.

My heart sank. Here, I will not have very much freedom. Ink will be my salvation.

I thought of the solace of cool water running over my wrists. I missed America, my homeland. Hometown speech would have been welcome...

Our first morning we drove into Parksville. Here it was. It had a lingerie store called Close To You, a large friendly thrifty, with signs like "It's not rain, it's liquid sunshine."

O

It's hard going away—hard coming home. Pascal-Christine, with her Quebec Catholic background, had discipline. She'd just packed up her mother's apartment almost single-handedly, was shipping us out a music stand, a china cupboard, a family chandelier and some Royal Albert China. Did I, Alexa-Sabine, look forward to the arrival of these things?

I could see her as a young nun, her curried head with dark bangs and bob bent over her reading. She was Easter in all seasons, "sun rising." She called me "heart rising" on the eve of going into our twenty-seventh year.

Out of the corner of my eye, I observed the family next door at the cabins—a man, a woman and two small boys who appeared the heart of the ordinary. As in my childhood, I had the shivers—the ordinariness of small towns horrified me, what I saw as the inadequacy of family love. Right down the road from us was Cobblestone Pub, Mr. Sweeper, Sure Copy Center, Julie Laviolette Realtor, Cash In A Flash and Color Your World Paint Shop plus a hot tubs factory, Tops Tree Service. Out the window was an autumn ocean, full of whitecaps. Thank heaven, we'd brought ocean clothing.

We were in a forest, our small backyard a patch of burnt dry grass, reminiscent of the desert. Why at this moment, did there shoot through my memory the phrase which was one of my favorite promises from *Psalms*, "With the Lord there is steadfast love, and with him plenteous redemption"?

Could I write here? Knowing ink to be the great cure.

Still shaken, we'd come in the wake of that horrific accident. The morning news had announced a traffic accident on the mainland five mornings ago, which killed three young men. Little did I know that one was the schoolfellow and playmate of my best friend's grandson. They'd known each other from pre-school through college. The young man had been driving with a buddy when the dump truck, fully loaded, lost control and slammed into them, setting them on fire.

Erin-Eileen, a Yorkshire woman whose family were from Ireland, with her tragic history. Hardly having dried her eyes from commemorating what would have been the forty-fifth birthday of her dead son than she learned of this disaster. I felt remorse leaving her in mourning but this holiday had been in place for so long, canceled in past years three times.

When Pascal and I drove back from the village of Parksville, I saw a quail, my first, from the corner of my eye in our bare backyard. A flood of quail in cockades and chainmail followed, like a lit match whose flame was gray and brown. Here was a whole brood!

Spiritually I took note, stiffening my spine. *I am not losing it!*, I reassured myself, slowed down as I have been lately, by my body. Erin's suffering still cast a pall over us, for sheer narrative hook, it held me.

The quail cast a contrasting light of redemption.

We would be content here—although each of us, Pascal and I, probably thought we had been battling the strife of my visible handicap so long.

Stark as our yard appeared at first, it contained a small world. Later that day we were to see deer, and one redheaded woodpecker in addition to a pair of large brown wild rabbits.

If my spirit snagged upon the fact that one step in front, one behind the cabin could block my entry to the world of this yard, I could flash the cabin world in my pocket mirror. Mirrored, the steps became ironed. Reflected fires cannot burn human flesh.

I look at sun torching bushes and think of a handsome face, a woman's—Roman Catholic, almost Roman in its severe discipline.

The Parthenon has no straight lines, because in nature there are no straight lines. The columns all curve a bit: continued upward, somewhere in the sky they'd meet. It is a temple to virginity, enclosing only the single sculpture of Venus, our virgin love. The Greeks say if you have a wounded heart, touch it as little as you would a wounded eye. I have been waiting since the first hard frost of last year.

The cabin room with warm Tudor panels, Proctor-Silex coffee maker, Black & Decker toaster. We photograph them—all the pictures are of what we want our lives to be: liquid and lovely. The fire burning in the mirror does not burn our skin, no.

At last, September will come; the world of the active body so insistently energetic will subside. Quiet. Falling apples, then the glow of October, the prolonged Indian summer before, at last the real prize: the austerity, the August austerity of winter.

Meanwhile the rabbit the color of a terra-cotta pot runs, and deer dart. "Close to you," whispers the nightshirt. Venus shivers in the Parthenon while the real lover hesitates to touch, to draw close.

Those three schoolboys made into human torches—what will they have to say if they ever cross over into the fields of Elysium? Where is their plenteous redemption?

Little escapes the demolition ball, the wrecker's circle. Gunsmiths have always got their velvets and stuffed pheasants. Here I sit in my Extra Large green tee-shirt, "Beach Acres" stamped on it, "The Great Canadian Outdoors." I, Sabine, whose counselor my last year walking, wrote in my autograph book, "I hope you will return next year to be best hiker."

○

Lace and the Way We Were—a local exhibit is written up in the local rag. A railroad runs through the small town at night flattening the miles with its Doppler. I'm reading about collieries in Britain, little changed from a century ago. I grieve that I am not driving the mountain we climb with the car.

I slip a piece of blank paper in, with carbon behind. This is the imprint of our life, this mirroring. We must love as though never hurt, sing as if no one can hear; dance as though heaven were right here on earth. One-by-one, here they come again—those quail, mother first, in the dusty heat of late afternoon bringing plenteous redemption and grace to the round patch, bleached with last hours of sun. A flood of quail follow, like the blur a struck match makes, a second time—a flood of heartbeats taking breath away as in morning.

I cannot wait 'til geese fly south in double V's, when my prairie friend will write, definitively, "Winter is here."

"No good Bavarian woman," her mother told her at sixteen, "would smoke."

When she left, I felt like a tree whose trunk had been split right down center: one half left dead, one dark and bleeding.

The second morning is overcast, dull, as though the world were a globe covered with gray Plexiglas. We decide on driving to Cathedral Grove.

Soon today's sun will set. It is getting further from its source, the heat. The cold comes. My father could not have led my life because he lacked vivid imagination, good doctor that he was. Plus he couldn't bear dirty hands and wheels always track dirt in. How he would kick at the traces of frustration! I lay my head forward on this improvised desk—sweatered arm, pushing the typewriter aside with my elbow. I see my blue sweater cuff turn darker, indigo. Tears, liquid sunshine.

It's ironic that Pascal and Erin-Eileen could try for the exact same Shakespearean role: a boy-bride, an Orlando. Both have low-pitched voices. Like Rosalind they could be outfitted as a man, wear doublet and hose. *As You Like It*, so sweetly deceptive: "One inch of delay more is a South Sea of discovery." The play's a teacher, dealing as it does, with the power of regenerative love: illusion and reality.

Like Pascal and Erin, both Orlando and Rosalind have good natures and are forced to flee, taking refuge in the Forest of Ardent. Pascal has me. Erin takes no refuge. Or only hints at one. Erin is like Rosalind in being educated, but female and in certain ways—no money, no marriage, powerless. Orlando is nobly born like Pascal but uneducated, unlike Pascal.

Stretched out on the desk is a flyer. I read the hiking flyer: "Come with us. Look down upon islands lying over a mile below. Alpine flowers. The snow peaks of the coast surround you."

Driving home from our aborted buffet, Pascal said, "It would have been fun."

"Can we drop the past? Look, Snow!" I pointed.

Our eyes swept upward to silver snow. I remembered considering trekking in Nepal. Oh be good, you two women, and enchantingly beloved.

But Arden is not blessed any more than the Parthenon which is a tribute to Virginity. Arden is a place where Icy Fang and churlish chiding of winter's wind chills the bones reminding people of frailty, human. And suggesting the tough lesson that hardship has sweet uses.

Touchstone has yet to learn the basic nature of honor. Oliver accepts the profound nature of shared hardship becoming closer. Closer? Or simply becoming more who one is. All at last emerge from the "winter of their discontent." I will not lose my lease with any I love. Erin has a violent background, Pascal a most civilized one. Pascal, more the poet, writes of the rising of the heart and that indeed is what we have. Yet, Erin sees a lion in her dream on a roof just opposite her which I interpret as strength staring strength down. Her gifts are few and far between: hard-driven, shriven.

April when we woo, December when we wed. "Maids are May when they are Maids, but the sky changes when they are Wives."

Erin-Eileen, bravely, even with a touch of tenderness, she chaperones her three grandchildren. Two of whom flew over from England for the funeral of their playmate—its rehearsal, all the proceedings.

I thought of her as we drove to Cathedral Grove. I'd waited years. We started early. Woke at seven, thinking I will finally get to see Cathedral Grove, those eight-hundred-year-old trees today. That heightened consciousness which is keen anticipation began the night before. I began looking forward to the drive when Pascal and I went to the shuffleboard court alight with twilight, glowing reddish. Three stands of old arbutus stood, knolls with sprouts of young trees. The park seemed to exist in another time, an earlier age. I watched children run and climb. I felt my own legs moving fast as those kids' legs moved, sun-browned in the tennis court next to shuffleboard. They whacked a tennis ball, neon green. I held the shuffle stick, thrust hard as I could to hit the circles of yellow and blue plastic but barely nudged them. Yellow would be mine, blue Pascal's. Pascal got into the swing her dark hair shining as though painted with light. Her five-foot-seven body brought her weight to bear upon the stick and shuffle as I never could. She shot a disc clear off the board.

"You're great at this!" I said.

"This is fun," she said. After twenty minutes she asked glowing, "want to play more?"

"But," I thought of saying, "I haven't really been playing."

Driving up to Cathedral Grove, I thought of shuffleboard. After a very long winding drive we came to MacMillan Park. In parentheses it was called Cathedral Grove.

"They want to keep it quiet," Pascal said.

We hadn't thought about parking. It was jam-packed! The lots full to both left and right side of the two-lane highway. This was a summer Monday, before noon. Some cars had double-parked.

"We may have to wait to see Cathedral Grove," I said, "but that's all right, I'm loving the drive. Look, a lake to our right, It's called Lake Cameron."

"I wonder what mountain we're climbing."

"Doesn't your map say?" I asked as the miles mounted, and the steepness sharpened.

"My map stopped."

"We need to find a safe turnaround."

"May take awhile."

Lake Cameron now lay far behind.

"I'd be delighted, you know," I told her, "simply to turn around. We could find the lake again and picnic in the car. I can see things from the car."

"That's what I'm trying to do. Ah—here we are."

"If only the map continued we could tell if the road loops back, we'd see what would happen if we continued."

"I'll find a turnoff. There's the lake again."

It was still the second morning of our vacation. We found a pull off.

"It's safe," said Pascal.

"I want to jot a few notes, then our picnic. Be careful going up the hill."

I saw her tall easy body loping down the hill which was rather steep to the water. I sat tight and prayed.

It was then that the man with the survey came, who gave me the yellow pencil with his questionnaire.

'Ma'am," he began, "May I take a moment of your time?"

"Depends."

"We're doing a survey of the area."

God had given me a voice, I was about to use it! Eagerly, I took the paper from his hand. My pencil began moving furiously. I said I'd never made it out of the car into one little sunlight square foot of their park and forest because there was no wheelchair parking. I added we lost the chance to picnic above Lake Cameron because those paths were too steep.

At this point, Pascal returned.

"Before we eat, you'd better check how we're to get out of here safely."

"Good idea," she said wandering off, returning fifteen minutes later.

"It's hard to tell," she said. "I went to the bathroom as well. I checked it for access."

"And?"

"Yes," she grinned.

I handed her a prosciutto sandwich. She pulled the top bread from the bottom at once. "I'm distributing the contents evenly," she said, and ate the sandwich.

Then we shared small green plums.

I thought of stopping at a hairdresser in Parksville on the way home since I couldn't manage the sink in the cabin. I recalled, we'd begun our trip with eight hundred dollars worth of car work, four new tires. That's when we'd begun this morning's trek with road construction right outside our cabins, and I, Alex-Sabine, had thought of turning back right then at the beginning...

"How would you feel about doing a small laundry when we get back to the cabins?" I said to her. "We're getting low."

"Laundry? Could I tomorrow?"

"Sure."

I thought of Erin-Eileen telling her two grown grand children on the way back from their schoolmate's funeral. "Sing out loud all the way back, you two, as you did when you were children."

○

The light grew thinner and thinner like tin. It looked like rain. I thought of plenteous redemption. As we passed the quaint crafts village, Coombs, Pascal asked, "Why don't we make Coombs our tomorrow adventure?"

"I might rather stay in the cabin and write. Let's just stop for a carrot cake on the way home."

"Let's!"

I felt myself on the verge of splurging at the bookshop, *Mulberry Bush*, nearby. Bookstore and cake, a browse.

"By the way," she smiled, "Did you mail that survey?"

"Which?"

"The one the park warden handed you."

"How could I? I will. Finally I got to speak my mind."

"But you should have just given it to me to drop in the wood box above Lake Cameron."

It was a relief to get out of the car, at Parksville Thrifty.

"Here, Alexa," Pascal said, handing me her bag with "Save the Earth and its Creatures" on it.

At Thrifty she grabbed a large basket.

"Not a large one," my heart sank.

I saw her piling cherries, limes, red peppers and green while I went to find a fruit cake. I thought of what might have been the magnificence of those eight hundred-year-old trees. I went with the cake into the *Mulberry Bush*. Here I found my splurge: the collected volume number one of C.S. Lewis' letters. From schoolboy days on, the war, Oxford. I opened one that said, "O fool!" and knew I was a goner. I hardly winced when the sales woman rang up the tab. "Ink is the great cure for all human ills," Lewis wrote within.

As we drove up to the cabin I said Emily Dickinson's poem to myself:

A certain slant of light winter afternoons

Oppresses like the heft of cathedral tunes.

Heavenly hurt is gives us...

We passed a trailer which read God's Iridology.

"What's iridology?" I asked Pascal, who explained.

Perhaps next summer we'd get to see Cathedral Grove when quinces ripened, and quilts turned all colors, going into our twenty-eighth autumn. Driving home, again we passed an autumn ocean with white caps even higher than when we'd driven out. I realized that I had been singing all my life as though nobody heard me.

I was dizzy with elation transferring from car to silver wheelchair. I discovered the yellow pencil that fell into my lap. "Look," I laughed, "That ranger's yellow pencil."

I had been given plenteous redemption.

Brown Rabbits: The Meek Shall Inherit the Earth

"Poor Maddie! with her ear-splitting voice, how she must have wept the second time not to have a boy!"

I wake to air mirror-still. Alexa-Sabine. No bird calls. The Doppler of the little E&N Railroad is silent (the Esquimalt to Nanaimo.) I rise careful not to wake the sleeping Pascal.

Drawing up the blinds I discover two brown floppy-eared wild rabbits who make it off, startled, into the bushes at the rattle of the back door opening. A dappled morning. Is that blue window in the sky to be my escape?

We are promised, by Corinthians no temptation beyond our power to escape—with the trail, we will be provided the way out.

This is the sixteenth day of August. We row toward what? Eternity, our blades making a small dent in the water...

When Pascal wakes, we will walk, the forest the only company that we have besides each other.

I wait for the quail's bubble from the bush. It begins in back of her throat.

How inherit the earth when, no matter how acceptant, earth seems to yield up less each day. But what you do have will be all the more holy—comes the counter voice inside me.

I never asked for the ecstasy to come from outside, as the bride receives it from her bridegroom. But what if I do soon?

Housekeeping phones. Do we want fresh sheets? Maddie, poor Maddie, with her ear-splitting voice: how she must have wept at her second birth to discover it wasn't a boy.

○

Our five red summer gerberas, in glass pitcher with handle, are three days old. The wood duck with yellow clothespin beak holding the menus stands still. I go to phone my relatives in the deep South, which is incongruous: they should never have gone.

This town, this cabin room, feels like *Silentville*. The Alabama Light & Power Co glowed near, was never far.

Dawn is my golden retriever of news: I hold still to receive the word. Autumn will come, steadying the blood, and reddening the ground East in Ontario, and the Northeast, our home. No New York Jewish family was meant to move far south of Boston.

○

"Hardship builds wisdom and character," I told myself while Pascal went into the bath. "Bathe for both of us," I called out.

"It's funny," she says, "There was a breeze, it's just dropped," taking off her white robe. Always there's a time during one's stay in the woods when one feels one has stayed too long. That's when you want to push the clock's second hand, wash your hair. Tomorrow Qualicum or Coombs. A Scottish name deriving from comb for sheep?"

"I am weary of you," Shakespeare's Orlando dared say.

"Heart hole—a hole where his heart should be since he shows no sign of having had his heart pierced by Cupid's arrow."

Two floppy brown rabbits began my day. I turn on the night light wishing for it to become evening which makes bearable, all things.

Pascal brings me a milkweed pod, breathing with care. "Look at all the tiny filaments, the delicate structure. I put a couple in the air and they float—they really just drift, their incredible delicacy!"

She will try to bring them home safely.

"You are lovely," Pascal says. "Have I told you—?" but her voice trails off.

I feel dusty, burned out. I long for the quail. Her hands like two brown rabbits come out and take mine.

Johnny Jump-Ups: Those Who No Longer Dream

One day, the Lord will summon us to his household and assign us to our rightful rooms.

That mansion will be in the sky. These cabins are on earth.

That time is far to come. I, Sabine, woke to Johnny Jump-Ups, a miraculous blue in our desserts last night, this morning like two dead insects, mosquitoes, I discovered near the map right under the reading lamp.

"Here," Pascal said, "I'm starting to dream once again."

"Had you stopped dreaming?"

It was Hamlet who said, "To be or not to be. To sleep, to dream. Aye, there's the rub—no more to dream."

○

Wildlife leaps through the picture window in the backyard. Pascal slips an old sweater over pajamas and goes with camera into the yard. The E&N Railroad fractures morning silence like shattering glass, scattering the last of my dream. In evenings it breaks the black as delicately as though night were fine eggshell.

"Alex, a red-headed woodpecker, come!" I come to her stage whisper.

It has become the sixteenth day which it was to be yesterday. This day promises that our sins, like scarlet, will become white as snow; that crimson shall become wool. The morning of scarlet and white, snow and yarn.

There *are* moments when I still hope the ecstasy, the shimmering, will come to me—like Holy Ghost—from outside, the way the bridegroom fills the bride...

As she shot the woodpecker, I began thinking of the mortal danger, the lethal one, we would live and breathe and lie down to sleep in if we did not dream. Not to dream would signify not to desire: dream is that realm where we can give ourselves all we want to spill over like cornucopia into both our hands, but which fails us in the world.

Only last night, I dreamed in these woods of a woman so bashful she had to speak to a tape recorder. First, I saw her in the room, then saw her being filmed as she spoke into an off-camera microphone. "Tell us," said the voice of an interviewer, "precisely what happens when you are close to someone."

"I," she spoke hesitantly in a whisper, gaining ground as she continued, "...first, I feel like withdrawing; then as they are near enough to touch—their skin frail as paper, I want to cry, 'let me out of here!' I fear I will hurt them."

I lost the rest of my dream. Our purpose in life: to dream.

Yesterday wearing the Big Canadian Outdoors shirt, forest-green, I phoned home. I've never seen "home." It's Texas now.

If we lost dream? Faces would become impassive, voices flat—not necessarily with a rich calm. Like in the former Soviet Union, the sky could become a soulless grey.

But where do the Johnny Jump-Ups come in?

With their blue, like passion, of a young nun.

Childhood needs secrets: adults do too. Sunset barking of dogs, lapping on water on sandy shores. On a wind and a prayer, the dead child, the son comes in on a white sailboat-into our lives again: the dead boy can whistle and dance! Listen!

Dream of India where laundry, in Bombay for example, is still an intense industry. Cotton cloth is boiled, blenched and beaten at open-air laundries. Across India, hand washing is the rule.

Growing up in Pennsylvania, coming of age I allow to happen in dream. Brush Valley, Tiny Brush Valley stretching just a mile between Brush and Nittany mountains. A dollar kept in the bathroom to separate saints from sinners. The world that cut-clean like the facets of a diamond.

This is where the Johnny Jump-ups came in: ultra-violet, put in homemade apple-pie last night, as blue as those Pennsylvania valleys.

"We'll take them home!" beamed Pascal.

Back in Pennsylvania, on wide, valley roads, horses would pull carts like toys. White was the most strict color.

This morning, the blue I stepped out to was breath-taking. I thought of being a railroad-buff, a train spotter. Watching at Bethlehem Steel railroad wheels take shape, red hot, cooling. Then wait 'til day's rail traffic started up at the roundhouse: a mystery undreamable almost. There was a one-room Blue Gate Amish school, off Black Mountain Road, named for the nearby farm's blue gate. With my sister, I would toss memories back and forth like an India rubber ball.

Alabama Light & Power Co

I woke with a start last night, realizing I'd been dreaming about the riffles in that Pennsylvania stream, where I summered in my eleventh year, in the Allegheny Mountains. Skies clearing. always, between truth and gossip, went the Amish young, shocking fields of ripe corn.

○

Earth would be a battlefield of dead bodies if we did not dream.
Our brief gaudy hour will have come and gone.
Forgiveness is a canceled debt.
But whom do we accuse? Who forgive?
We have all eaten, salted our crow.

What's hard is staying on, staying kind when you no longer feel needed, nourishing. So, I dream my way back to Big Valley Road, clopping horses pulling Amish buggies with tops of all colors, white the most severe. No adornment. If the Amish didn't agree with each other, what did they do? Now, I'm entering the field of dream of my earliest time: pupils march to the front of the class to do sums, count syllables, spell. Their eyes are clear; some are vacant.

There is an explosive crash when a big tree falls. There are glowing red Bessemers fired up all along the Allegheny River Valley.

○

But here where Pascal is and I am, kids line a sinkhole. "Me too!" shouts one boy, the most sunburned, thinnest and bravest—the one they slipped that "Angel Dust" to that night at the party; that night which was Erin's son's last night on earth. He was nineteen. He never saw twenty.

She speaks each morning to her dead son. His picture is the one she sees first on waking.

"But I rarely dream of him, you know," she said last week before Pascal and I left on vacation.

"Seriously?"

"Seriously. Only I did have that dream of the rope-colored lion sitting on the roof opposite me. Now, what do you think that means?"

"That you're brave. That you took your grandchildren to the funeral and said, 'Mind you sing all the way home, as you did when children.' That you can face your fear down."

One day, do you believe you will be rejoined with your son?

One day the Lord will summon us to his household. Then we will have plenteous redemption. The light will not be jump rope skimpy, thin. He assigns us to our rightful rooms. For the time being, watching brown-eared rabbits, culling Johnny Jump-ups, we remain.

High Kicks

"I have the coldest wrists at night"
 Mark Kipness with Kathryn Rantala
 unpublished collaboration *Candelaboration*

For Kathryn Rantala,
 for Anne, the child who couldn't sleep,
  & for "Amelia"

The fast in Silentville has turned into a feast, albeit a strange type leak.

The Coldest Wrists

I am fighting the refugee battle.

Amelia's thin wrists were coldest at night. Amelia, when she was a ballerina, child protégé of the Bolshoi Ballet Academy, was adored. When she danced, her leg was drawn up as if with an invisible silk thread in the sky, in a perfect six o'clock extension. She felt like a marionette. There was a silence of the cells. She herself possessed a Giacometti, Modigliani elongation—Sephardic?

A Jewish girl with charcoal almond hazel eyes and jet blue-black hair, granddaughter of Romanian gypsies, she was born in the South, with a magnolia complexion and blue-white skin. She dwelt in a swirl of silhouette girls, mainly children her age, twelve or a bit older, translucent as lit wax. Candlebration. She lived among a world of shadow gymnasts dong calisthenics and pretzels. This was a transparent circus which was dream and nightmare combined. She remembered the applause, bouquets, being in the quiet darkness bathed in moonlight, when the limelight shone upon her.

Burned like a lithograph into her, the precise moment she had begun dying. Emotionally exhausted, Amelia heard her athletic coach teacher say, "You will be practicing enough when you hate it." She had been born to be a gymnast, she discovered first at age nine in France and then when she got a small part at the Jewish Community Center. All the gold in Florence could not outshine her.

"She has a glow about her," my sister Belle said. Amelia told me over the phone, "I have had a bit of luck Aunt."

Amelia's passion matured at age twelve when she auditioned for the Bolshoi and they took her unconditionally granting her a full scholarship. They auditioned her telling her to perform a few simple movements: jumping, extensions, twirling.

"I want to be a dancer, Aunt," she told me, thrill in her voice, "even when I'm a grandmother. I don't ever want to stop workout, the balance beam."

She was enrolled in the summer gymnastics school and took to it as a bird to air. Her mother and father decided she could go back to the boarding school for a year. Wasn't she too young, I asked? She had to give up a lot: eating desserts, running with other kids, social life. She had to get used to having bleeding toes once she went on point. She had to practice before mirrors both holding the bar and standing free. The rigorous discipline. A pre-adolescent child of twelve, graceful as an adolescent Dante.

She made herself brave every time her parents visited and left. A bit tight emotionally to begin with, as her father perceived, Amelia coiled up like a snake. Was the fieldstone facade of the ballet academy not somewhat desolate? Parents were required to fax permission for the few allowed outings to the 7/11 down the street, weekend's treat.

She remembered the light fall when the clock stopped. There was stone and ice. Where she had woken in a state of elation, how she woke panic-stricken and by: four p.m. that December afternoon, nightfall had begun to come into her blood and bones. She had been stretching about this rudiment, an elegant beauty. She had just turned fourteen. She exited this body, the moment etched into her blood, burned in. She had just danced the final exams of the Bolshoi ballet, her right foot extended to six o'clock of the sky. She held it there for five seconds, then let it down, let all the breath out of her earthly frame in a blue light like Picasso's harlequins, his blue period. Her house was a body whose door she had exited. She had loved a lover and given him over.

Teal breath had hung before in a crystal cloud, walking she wore her black winter coat collar up about her ears, in December when the head mistress at the Ballet Academy had said, "You are the future Olga Korbut and Nadia Comenici combined." She had been one of the great dancers of the century, the century past. She thought of the iced Thames in one of the forty winters when it froze solid. A voracious reader—Amelia imagined frost fairs, her very her own in her fantasy, tents strung up glittering in the frost, iridescent underneath a mother-of-pearl sky, with her prima ballerina, taking their breath away, the women and men bundled against the chill, making the exquisite bow the Bolshoi teachers has taught her a curtsey with many folds and complex movements.

She identified with Amelia who flew alone across the Atlantic, goggles, and bravery her profile. "I'm emotionally exhausted," she draped her fourteen-year-old body over a chair and said, "Amelia is Belle's second self," grandmother told me.

Burnout, which had smoldered, ignited in an instant. She gave herself little cigarette burns. She slept days. She paced all night. She skipped classes at the Montessori school. They home-schooled her the year she was thirteen rather than board her again at the Bolshoi. She had experimented with alcohol with the other fourteen-year-old girls. She experimented with speed. She went through a slow, slow recovery, no longer brought the house down. A star, when a star crashes it smolders, then turns to crumbled ash. She stole a silk scarf from a local boutique with another girl. Her mother didn't know what to do with the scarf. Her father thought he should ask Amelia return it and pay in work hours at the store. Her mother thought to burn it. They hid it instead and finally put it in the bin. Her mother taped all Amelia's phone conversations with a mini recorder placed in the phone dial, disguised, so that she could catch ever word of that tense, piping child voice in her confidences. For the time, there was only freeze between mother and daughter.

○

Amelia, however, survived. The bloodbaths had purged her of some of the horror and sorrow of relinquishing that gift she was given at birth. Now at twenty, Nikon slung over her shoulder, she stepped into a New York City morning. She noted the grains of light in each stone pore. Did this call for a shot? She cautiously slid the lens in its felt case from her backpack and attached it, the macro. Nests within nests safe kept her instruments, her precision tools as precise as the dance had been. She felt the weight of her slight body pulled a bit to the right, then took twenty shots from twenty angles.

She was slight and born with scoliosis which didn't show up until age thirteen. Her mother took her to two yoga teachers, a chiropractor and a Chinese herbal medicine and acupuncture expert. "All three of her curves are corrected," Belle phoned thrilled when x-rays were taken months later of what had been, at age nine, the perfect set of bones. Still Amelia was burned out, perhaps as a result of all the corrective measures taken. As her back had leaned, her vision leaned now.

One day when they were alone, four gymnasts bullied her. "Amelia, your hair is too long, your bun was too heavy." She began to see herself as an ugly duckling. She felt her eyelids weighed with lead. She traveled slowly through the long corridors of the academy and took the stairs up to the roof. She was found on the academy roof crying silent tears.

With the long-handled spade of her tongue, one of the ballet masters cuffed her 'til Amelia was a scroll, like parchment, thin gray translucent child made to stand on one foot—like in France—her face to the wall. Berlin…Berlin…Sleeping with the enemy. She had hooked up with a German photographer, raised in Munich. The exotic drew her once more. Might she stand at the bar once more under Berlin skies and do that high extension on soil where her ancestors were cremated alive, performing the most eloquent act of a rebel angel?

As she shot the New York stone, luminous as human flesh, in photographic frames the film unfolded of her mother bent over box after box, packing and packing all the family's belongings. Twice they bought and sold a house due to her. They sold the home in Denver, a huge undertaking, and moved first to Tucson, which also failed, but then to a New England township, scrubbed white by the sea as if by soap, or silver as if polished with wax.

The tarnish stood only in embossed edges in this salt-sea village with a white needle-steeple, a town where at last something worked for Amelia, a private school for the arts, both boarding and non-boarding. She lived at home in a small house half of which her mother rented for them. Belle set little votive candles before a fireplace she didn't light. She hid the Gillette razors. Amelia went to many psychiatrists, was finally given medication. "My last resort," Belle said. "But it makes a real difference, I can see the mood lift in her."

The Thames frozen, she froze, her bun was no longer, she cut it all off and was growing back a Saint Joan, boy-soldier cut at age fourteen after chopping off the tresses. She wore earth-boots and thick red socks.

She had put on weight. "And you know her," my sister confided. Thin as a rail, she was developing a boyish woman's body, long wrists bony, cool, and thin.

Cast in gray iron, the fourteen-year-old appeared, kin to the molten sky. Jarring, a dog barked in the courtyard. Then the earth healed up with silence. "Amelia! Amelia!" the girls taunted because they were envious, she was the best. Yet in her own dark eyes, the mirrored world of Amelia made her unpopular. She was ugly in her eyes. Her anger thinned to a runnel of icy water from a faucet, leaving an iron-red stain along the zinc sink. Blood. Wrath could run too as a cold stream. Sorrow was a deeper emotion, underneath the anger. There all the tension, the drama relaxed, relented.

Walking the three blocks in Greenwich Village to photography class this December morning, the words blew back in her face like the first chill winds of autumn turning to winter, "Dance 'til you hate it… 'til your feet are bleeding."

Painting, then sculpting, then photography was the next pattern. She thought, we were together in a familiar place in a world off kilter. She thought. We'd get it level again, the way we do everything, by sheer force of will power. Daddy turned ballistic when she burned her belly… "I'm sorry, daddy," she told him many times. Every relapse made him desperate, desperate.

Dancers had become translucent, arms legs, like the photographs she now developed under the red darkroom light bulb. She loved photography. But morbidity continued to float about like radium in the bones. She had hooked up with a young German photographer and he became her lover in Berlin. Now did she think, she could reach out to the other side of pain, of being a star crumbling, turning to gray ash? Round-eyes when frightened, she had almond eyes when relaxed. In this strange, post-enemy territory she was challenged to dwell in a window cut in history, the Holocaust museums, the war ruins still about her and within her, she did one last high kick with Lenni in her dream. Did she dream of the Munich mannequins? What if she became a ballerina again in Berlin?

Absolutely, Amelia had an out-of-body experience when she gave up gymnastics. She rose above her body and saw it not on a white stretcher, but doing a perfect score of ten. Like the Phoenix, child-Lazarus rose from the fire: she came to life again, although weeks before it the morning had arrived, the morning she decided to bleach her hair. "Make me blond," she had said squaring her shoulders, entering the quiet beauty shop at an early hour, stepping lively raising herself to her full five-foot three. "I have the cash," and sat watching her rippling chestnut waves of hair fall to the floor in the barer shop in Tucson.

She recalled it with the shivering thrill she felt when she'd first lit up, each inhalation exhaling some of the tension coiled in her lithe, light body. Her first orgasm made her so cold she lay, holding thin wrists, hugging her spectral, orphaned frame for hours 'til she calmed. It wasn't with a boy, she gave herself permission to do this alone but not until age seventeen. The performing élan and energy, nonetheless, had no egress. Pale as a white egret, Amelia stood poised in the bedroom doorway, now not after self-injurious little cigarette burns, but after orgasm. Again, startled, fearful.

Then, when she was fourteen, there had been no where for her to go but into the stainless steel where it fit with a horrifying, perfect fit and came out with scarlet dramatic gash then a forecast of menstrual blood which would be the natural red iron. Despite the pain it was less than the pain she felt within. High kicks turned low volume like dirges in her brain, she continued walking in the Manhattan early winter morning. Her wrists were chill and thin. Like the rare rose of Calcutta, blood had opened and flowered.

O

I, her aunt half way across the world, remember the morning in July over half a century ago when I too nearly died. My nemesis struck from a black winged creature, a fly, perhaps settling on the forefinger of my right hand when I pointed to something, then set finger to lip, perhaps landing on the rim of a water glass in summer's first heat, early July. I weighed 52 pounds when they lowered me, stiff, on a board to the floor where the scale was located. Terrified, I looked up so far from icy yellow-tiled floor up to the ceiling. I'd read about Michelangelo on his back on a scaffold painting the Sistine Ceiling between 1508 and 1512. It was only one week after the acute phase of polio. My parents had answered my incessant questions what I had by telling me I had a cold of the central nervous system. What was that cylindrical silvery shape in the corner of my hospital isolation room? Unearthly, after worldly? Might it be part of death and resurrection? My cousin and her best friend, the quiet, schizophrenic, insomniac child, Magritte knew what I had before I did. My legs grew thin as wrists over the next few months. I was a boy girl soldier with blond hair and coke-bottle green eyes. I wanted to talk with Amelia about my twelve years. Will we ever get to the point where we can talk about this? Was it her child who could dance a replacement of her sister whose legs were taken away?

My high kicks still came but were now verbal leaps. Always a word-child and gymnast, I transferred, translated leaps across gym floors and dance floors into syllables when I began writing, singing myself to sleep and now, nearing seventy, my own heart armoring is breaking, after seven decades my frosted Thames. I look down at thin wrists; I was the seven-year-old child who saw Nijinsky, the mad Russian at Jacob's Pillow, summer 1946. He did do high jumps and hover in the air for seconds. I no longer drink, not a jot. No lime sliced artistically into tonic and gin. No scotch on the blue-crystal rocks. But I think of lighting up a Sobranie, I miss the woody smell and feel, and then slip them into the drawer again. Candelbration.

Now all has become ice, while Annike is a kind of evangelist for my works urging Sweetheart and me to celebrate St Andrew's day since Sweetheart is a Scot. How high does one kick when all one's dreams come true? How low sink when they crumble to ruin? My thin legs are cold to the point of pain and my wrists are still chill, not only at midnight but throughout the day as I wheel, cart-wheeling with words, under a winter, shrift sun.

Amelia's Dreams

I became indescribably mournful, for I felt that this little corner on the face of the world, and the people who live in it, have a peace and dignity from which we are shut for ever.

John Millington Synge on the Aran Isles, Ireland

Was Amelia a dry drunk after she gave up ballet? She continued to dream but waking that she was Amelia Earhart, crossing the Atlantic, but it was in a tiny plane as she zoomed between talking head and talking head at, say, a party, a reception for her parents. Antique satin drapes, her Latin reader she carried in her waking dreams. Was her soul like the Aran Isles in Ireland, barren, unbearable insolated, dignified? Her mother Belle felt a bone-connection with the child and her suffering was beyond telling. The girl intuited this and internalized it. The full brunt of the storm arrived in her fourteenth autumn and felt like nails biting the face.

Nail-bitten but invisible mother and child bore themselves like figures in a Greek tragedy. No slight deviation had any effect upon this vast impact. It was, in that way, like a severe storm off the Nova Scotia coast. Whereas residents in a storm's path can flock to grocery and hardware to stock up on supplies like flashlights, storm lanterns and dry beans, Belle and Amelia had no where to turn. They turned smiling to guests at a reception and each woman saw the storm, like through a small isinglass windowpane to a stove, roaring behind the other's breastbone. The storm rocked each woman's capacity to breathe and circulate blood. Hands and feet blue each climbed under the covers that autumn in New England. They woke bright as the sky, but overcast with doom by mid afternoon. Even as sodium streetlights turned on in Provincetown, wind beat up against white washed clapboard saltboxes of homes, throwing salt at panes, and each knew there was no place but the other to turn. Locked up in a blitz with a daughter, that was the room inhabited by my sister Belle for the duration. In meteorology this is called high wave action, and volunteers can stand by. In such a crisis, there is no one. Heavy snowfall warning for Labrador means a heavy snowfall will be expected in Churchill Falls. A limit is called—upper limit—to destruction. In domestic tragedy, there is none.

So without a limit, I saw girl and parent flying like Amelia against a blinding storm. And that way, Amelia saw herself, remarkably with goggles strapped on, leather gloves, feet booted, body strapped into cockpit. She was alone sailing over the frozen Thames.

No frost fairs lit up that, her fourteenth winter following autumn. She walked the streets of the town home, head bent, ears covered by black coat collar, slender boy-girl chest taking the brunt of the knife winds. Her father and sister were far away, holding the frost of what had been home.

"How can you over-invest in a self-mutilating child?" Seth, Belle's husband's words, bit my dreams too. They were like a chainsaw biting into wood. None of us were safe, not with psychiatrist, medication, or embrace but we could be armed.

Amelia studied art, Van Gogh in particular who was suicidal like her. A little-known work by Dutch painter Vincent Van Gogh is being exhibited publicly for the first time at the Van Gogh Museum in Amsterdam. She read of a painting discovered after many years. Perhaps her life would be like this, in *jaune*, yellow, now her favorite color where periwinkle was in her tenth summer and burgundy in the winter she began pressing cigarette burns into her left arm, self-injuring with a series soft small burns. She clipped it out of the paper:

A Loving Couple has been kept in private collections for decades and shows a man and woman leaning towards each other while walking on a path next to a canal, her arm over his shoulder. Painted in March 1888, two years before his suicide, it's a small part of a larger canvas Van Gogh discarded because he didn't like what he had created.

A Loving Couple (1888) by Dutch painter Vincent Van Gogh is a small piece of what remains of a larger canvas the artist discarded as a failure (Van Gogh Museum/Associated Press).

"He cut it out carefully and kept it, so there must have been some element, something special that he saw in it," said Nienke Bakker, a researcher from the museum who helped to organize the display. The exhibit is a tribute to Van Gogh's friendship with French painter Emile Bernard.

Van Gogh described his ideas for the painting to Bernard in a letter. "I am sending you a little sketch of a study that is preoccupying me," Van Gogh wrote. "Sailors coming back with their sweethearts toward the town, which projects the strange silhouette of its drawbridge against a huge yellow sun."

A reproduction of the sketch is displayed next to the painting.

The sketch contains notations of the colors van Gogh intended to use, down to the word "jaune" — French for "yellow" — on the man's hat. The canal water is emerald green, as Van Gogh had planned.

The painter would eventually do more canvases portraying the same bridge outside Arles, France, from different perspectives.

Van Gogh started painting at age 27 but was largely unrecognized for his talent during his lifetime, save for a few friends and his brother Theo.

The artist, who suffered from debilitating bouts of depression, at one point cut off his ear.

He died of a self-inflicted gunshot wound in 1890 at age 37.

Amelia pasted this news clipping on the wall above her computer and had one of her nighttime dreams: she was cut so deeply nobody could suture the gash. It was on her abdomen where she always cut. Her moods were low as the last leaves of December scuttling on the ground. "They are," she wrote, "like rats scraping across glass into their prison."

I discovered her in my pre-dawn nightmare. We linked like hoops or circles on Boolean algebra. Electric shadows and magnetic zeros. I put my arm around her. She was fourteen. "I know," I said in as soft a whisper as illness creeps into the body and then out, "I know about the burning."

"They told you?" she shot up her dark eyebrows.

"Yes. I too had my addictions."

"What, Aunt?" "I wrote all the time to run away from a body that could not move. I felt frozen."

"Like the Thames?"

She told me about the frost fairs. "I dreamt them," she said, then smiling, "I drew them."

"That's marvelous!"

"I even..." she hesitated, "thought of photographing them."

"But how would you? How could you, Amelia?"

"First I'd draw what I saw in my dreams, then take out my Nikon."

Even in these early days she had sought and found the release of photography.

I did with my poems.

She drew one sheet of frosty tracing paper out of a drawer like those in old printer's trays only this was a map of her soul. It was etched with lines intersection. "They are villages, you see?"

"I see," I said.

As poet and photographer we turned the lens of imagination, trained upon these exquisite small drawings akin to botanical drawings.

Amelia's dreams had led me to reconsider Audubon. I said to her, "Do you know the ornithologist? Audubon?"

"Yes, he was a half breed. He killed birds to study them."

Silence fell between us like a knife, but then softened to a snowfall silence. I lit the fire—in Belle's grate—that night and for hours, until dawn, when I wakened, I dreamed my arm was about my younger niece's back, and she was not sobbing. She was staring, staring into the flames of Gin.

"How did you stop?"

"I realized it was do or die. Cold turkey, then I had a relapse and then slowly, slowly I worked through recovery. For the longest time after I met

Sweetheart, I longed to be taken care of. My childhood hospital experience overwhelmed me."

I thought to myself how she came to me with a knife and a ring, a ring to marry, a knife to protect. Soldier-girl. Amelia was the child whom grandmother had called the dwarf when three because she had the longest hair every seen on a three year old, by grandmother at least. The girl who she said, "has not got much from the neck up," looking at me, eyes shining.

"I had the people I love to consider."

"Yes, I know," she said. I thought of the map of girlhood unscrolled, revealing the world, then scrolled back again.

I now saw weavings in the fire, not only my own polio past. Coming out of that strange cold of the central nervous system my parents had lied to me about, but the lovely haunting insomniac and schizophrenic child Magritte who had loved me.

"Yes," she nodded. I watched the firelight play on her incredibly long ash-colored eyelashes, sweeping up like a prow of a ship. The storm cut a wide swath but now a path, a sea-lane of indigo was clear, rough waters blown all around like birds feathers. Icarian. There was a silence of the cells. O deliverance Lourdes. Still her mother could not cry. It was late night now. Soon it would be dawn.

The fire popped.

"You danced Anne Frank," I tried, gently, taking a jab at the Berlin love affair.

Electric lights and barbed wires, Jewish people standing naked, the SS.

"I know."

"How did you feel?"

"Wonderful. It was wonderful to play with my mother."

Someone threw a piece of soap at Auschwitz prisoners, they grabbed it like food.

I looked into the child's hazel-green brown eyes.

"It was the height of human sadism, Amelia," I said.

Cold dirt. Freeze.

Were those bakeries or brick factories at Terezin? "No people were burned in them."

"I know."

You know all this, you pretty little thing, you Audrey Hepburn flirt and still you go to Germany, you have fallen in love with a German. How low can you have fallen?

Stone and ice. Spring 1945. Weather eased a bit but mud got deeper. Those at Terezin were to move on.

"I was homeless," she whispered, "In Spain. I always had to move on. I only cut when my mother came."

"I know," I answered her.

Mengele, I thought, most feared. Organized cruelty. I wanted to express my hatred of the oppressors The death factories with trains full of Jewish people arrived hourly, days got shorter, the gas ovens were going days and nights, the air now full of smoke. The Nazis would have pushed me off a terrace: I was in a wheelchair. For a moment I wanted to throttle her, Amelia, this child who had caused Jewish blood to flow, the first cuts sharpest. The buildings were becoming ruins. I saw the embers housing them for some silent moments between us. The SS guards, the ballet academy, the head matrons, the sound of guns were always around us, within us.

"You know," saying to her, cupping her chin in my hands, tilting it up in firelight, "I nearly died at age twelve."

"I did too," she said in a husky voice, drawing a cigarette out of her jeans pocket.

"Mother, did she tell you about the day my jeans smelled of gasoline?"

"No!" I said, almost shouted, terrified. "What did you do?"

"I did NOT soak them in gasoline to set myself afire," she said fiercely. I spilled some, at a gas station when Hubert stopped to fill up. I was dating him then."

"My God, Amelia. How horrifying."

"I know," she said. She was the Southern night, magnolia, dripping with sweetness, nubile, not long before she'd be marriageable.

I looked at this solemn, magical, smoky child—so marriageable soon and felt immense anger and sorrow combined. One cannot over invest but one can spoil.

The sky was choked with snow, she womaned her small plane. I turned to her. She to me saying, "I am flying, Aunt and..."

"And," I completed the sentence watching the fire quiet like thousands of small cities, "you will land."

The Sweater: Treading the Rim of Medicine

The Garment

For half a century, Indigo began, I, the kid Mother called the Alabama Light & Power Co. itself, the girl with the sky's color in her name, I, the child who could no longer walk, have been treading precariously the rim of medicine haunted by polio: paralysis, poetry, the crystal terror (for polio resembles a crystal under the microscope.) I have been searching for a sweater, the one I was brought home in from State Hospital the winter I was twelve. Although it was over half a century ago, vividly I still see the cobbles of Montreal, rounded stones like loaves of bread coated with ice. What a bleak and icy Province, Quebec! Daddy had told me about the night train from Berlin to Munich when he was a young psychologist. I pictured it to be like this winter.

Dead winter, 3 a.m. of our lives: Maman, Danielle and I. Paralyzed from the waist down, I still remembering hugging trees and giving my legs burn, rope-climbing hand-over-hand climbing down from the gymnasium ceiling. Quick as a fox, with my eyes green as a coke bottle and my fox-red hair, I'd hit the rails. "*Foxfire*" was my nickname.

On my weekend pass home, I was determined not to tell Maman the cruelties the therapists inflicted on us: leaving us over the barrel with a chemical hot pack on our spine. The coils kept heating and heating 'til it burned the flesh. I screamed and shook it off one time. This treatment reminded me of the Maggies in Ireland who slaved in the Magdalene Laundries.

November 1951, I came home in a wheelchair, yet my new pullover freed me to reclaim my climbing body. I ran my hands over the wool. I was out of regulation hospital gown for the first time since I'd been taken in to Montreal City Hospital months ago, back in that steaming, hallucinatory summer night when everything appeared steeped in glass of silver ambulance July 2, 1951. The driver had a knife to perform a trach if I stopped breathing. I didn't need a tracheotomy but my best friend Margie had one. It leaves a little circular scar on the throat. Driven in, I was not yet aware of the hardships we'd be made to endure, the stoicism expected of children. Like all children I was part curiosity, part agony. More than garment, it was grail. Severe, scarring experience preceded and followed.

That first night home, I caught my profile in the mirror propelling myself in the pre-World War II wooden wheelchair. Danielle-Rachel flashed me a smile full of metal.

"Red fox," Mother tousled my auburn bob. I'd begun life as a dirty blond. A Buster Brown with bowl haircut. I looked like a gymnast who'd had a bad fall. We kids taught each other tricks to circumvent the sadism of the nurses and doctors. For one, I'd learned to smoke in a stairwell from my stretcher with a teen from another ward. She was in a Reese jacket.

Scientists bent above microscopes. "My first polio!" Mother heard the young pediatrician claim outside the lab.

Soldiers in the 1940's dressed in civvies intoxicated with freedom: smoking, eating chocolates, women. We had our *copines*[2]. our buddies, in our ward slang. Emaciated, we were dished up government surplus. Was there no nutritionist? We adored our night matron, tall form looming, and archangel, Madame Gabrielle, her shift knocking in just as twilight fell over that brick and limestone prison. The day-matron was discipline itself; she was chatelaine who held keys to the hospital's soul. "Bedpan, Strongin! Bedpan, Di Stefano!" she'd bark, hitting a skinny butt with an icy silver bedpan at 5 a.m. How does the body memory let this go?

O

The December night my parents drove me to the ancient brownstone 619 Rue Champagneur in the Jewish Quartier of Montreal, *flocons de neige*[3] wooly fresh snow had just begun falling. The Bastille had receded in the car window, its long wings in the shape of a cross. Mother Clothilde (indeed woman of the cloth) drove me home, my eye keenly shaved on the rearview capturing that jail, grey stone glowing. It was the first time I, a powerless child, had the power to put it behind. With one turn of the ignition, one hour of road behind us, the concentration camp for children dropped off earth. Yet children struggle both to hold onto memories, and to let them go.

My sweater felt velvety. Fifty pounds I weighed, on the flip side of puberty, complexion of the child on Yardley soap, I'd got a gamine appearance that would follow me into my sixties—an ironic gift of having given up half my body at age twelve?

On the ward, they called me greased lightning; it wasn't the boy left in me—that was the girl!

---

2   *Copine* is the patois, slang, for buddy. (*Copin* the male version.)
3   *Flocons de neige* means snow flakes.

Alabama Light & Power Co

I learned a handful of passwords to get me by the gates—the hospital Grail. Back home, there was the smell of chicken soup simmering on back of the stove in our windowless shoebox kitchen, "Do you want a backrub, child?" our neighbor, Griselle asked. I shook my head. Returned we were to the hospital precisely 48 hours after we left, or our beds ran out, huge threat because then who would keep us? Wards of the Province. Sunday night the hospital reclaimed body and soul, a bottomless pit opened which we'd plunge down like the screaming figures in *Guernica*. Abandoned again. I'd exchange sweater for board-like gown. Tomorrow morning, the Hubbard tanks, the tilt-table, the agony of limbs in spasm stretched. But we whispered not a word of this to our parents.

O

In my dream, summer turned into a frozen pool; a skater dipped into it like a firefly breaking ice-skin. Back in ward, "A 1, girls, non-spastic," I lay with my buddies, *mes copines*.[4] I'd earned a bald spot round as an egg in back of my auburn hair: the badge of the non-ambulatory child. Outside the ward window, a pool left by rain, multiple shimmering silver pools, mercury-bright, winter's mirrors. A miner's lights. I was put on the tilt table, onto which we paralyzed kids were strapped, a wheel of wood under it raising the body a few degrees each day toward a right angle with earth: the tingling in our legs as circulation returned was excruciating. Of course, like with the chemical hot packs over barrels, we were left alone and often the timer buzzed without a therapist heeding it, hence we were forgotten in these treatments. I thought of the Maggies again. The comparison with the medieval world came to me: traction, pulleys, and hoists. Later came the German brace shop in the hospital bowels, with its stench of dead leather and nails. Leaves were changing, Would I be paralyzed when winter came?

"Bedpan, Toscin!" I was wakened with the echo at 5 a.m. with the slap of metal. Smells of ammonia and burnt toast mingled with cocoa. The coca was a thin trickle into which we dipped toast to nourish bodies like those out of Dachau. Nurses sleek as oiled seals barked names, a drill of the infant military. What did they imagine, that we'd escape during night?

---

4   *Copine* is the patois, slang, for buddy. (*Copin* the male version.)

Lynn Strongin

O

Our lives, Clothilde's, Danielle's and mine, were monastic. Heading into the fifties felt like heading for hell. Autumn came and drenchers of Quebec rains. Ancient geographies were hauled up from the hospital basement musty and damp with warped and scarred maps of India and Spain. These were first published around 1900, re-published during the dirty thirties. These enchanted me. Europe forty years ago captured on shiny, clay-based papers whose celadon greens were oceans, lemon-yellows deserts, faded aqua for the world's inland waterways, Prussian blue for Lake Huron and Champlain. The St Lawrence waterway was teal. This touch of color created *bas-relief* to gray after Hubbard tanks, bone-wrenching treatments for poliomyelitis, the tenement house of medicine. Cartloads of families were plinthed in. "Two useless legs," Dr. Pain would proclaim at the foot of my bed, holding my metal clip chart in hand and frowning. Maps of the world bent from old hospital cellar-floods popped and crackled as we bent them open from in their waterlogged condition. This was how eighth-grade began.

Bringing Bright Honor Home

We emerged as they wanted us: tough as soldiers. I no longer had the washboard chest of my eleventh summer. I wore my hair in an Italian boy bob.

Hospital nights return when I see the mirror capture and hold a silver circle. Which is harder? The struggle to let go hospital memories as a child? Or the struggle to hold on? People tell me I have what Hart Crane calls the eternal northern eyes, with the sadness of Pierrot.

In Rue Bauchelard, I relive incendiary evenings worthy of Caravaggio. There'd been little sensuous to my world that twelfth year.

To a pilot handling a low-flying plane, our Bastille must have looked like a cross with hundreds of windows: long wing intersecting short wing, like some photographs of Dachau I've seen. Behind our grilled windows, the light that burned was too dim to read by. After the master switch was thrown, we used flashlights. Children of the ward and war. The glint of my red hair gave me away when I moved.

I cannot leave illness behind, but its memories leave me sometimes. *Au Revoir, mes copines!* We made cats' cradles with string, leaning forward in old-fashioned wooden wheelchairs—foot pedals touching another kid's. Every week, my anticipation of being driven home from the hospital intensified at 4:30, the last gym. Friday afternoon, I imagined the dingy gray milk light pouring in to be a church light, some shaft of dark sun. Thin as a Holbein girl, I'd be lifted, a war heroine from a burning plane on the silver-screen. The hero and heroine were my French-Canadian Catholic mother and my father, a thin, dark Jewish angel. I was a *Quebecois*. A Quaker who kept a straight spine. Taught to "think sparsely" like the Mennonites.

"You are the strength," Mother Clothilde said when we thought I might marry and have children. "Teach your children that although small, they are not voiceless, powerless beings."

I relive her words as I look at tonight's winter sky above L'Hopital Frontenac always delineated in my memory. My night suddenly darkened to clay colors, colors Giotto would dream. Colors to die for.

Life will suddenly turn back, just like that, like snapping your fingers. One sheet of mica peeled back to reveal December sky-scape of L'Hopital Frontenac. Then I begin rummaging in the wood bureau for the sweater I wore that night. Today visiting an Irish friend who spoke about the Maggies I heard her hunger pains, from radiation. "I'd got burned. It tore my stomach's linin'. All that radiation for cancer." I saw scar-grafted-on-scar. Like my own exposure to cruelty.

○

Half a century ago, I was lifted out of the car into an old wooden wheelchair leftover from World War II. We drive up to a strange new address, Rue Champagneur, its cobbles glossed with ice and moonlight, where my Mother Clothilde found us the apartment in the brownstone, It had a round bedroom where I told my kid sister Danielle about smoking. We plugged in the old victrola in the valise. I began playing jazz and swing.

Outside, it had stopped snowing. The air sparkled like salt. *Etincellante*[5]. I could feel the shadows closing in on me. I knew that soon my weekend-pass would expire. I'd be returned to rounds reminiscent of a text illustrating medieval life: egg-like nested tenements, wheels, sprockets, levies, an abandoned theme park in the ice.

"Danielle!" I laughed all of a sudden, "Run outside and scoop me up some snow."

"I can?" she smiled, her mouth flashing metal. "Look at me, Toscin!" she laughed running for both of us.

Bundled in a windbreaker I'd never seen, she dashed outside our ground floor apartment. She made faces outside the window scooping, with red mittens; enough snow to make a snowball, which she threw at the window. When it exploded we laughed.

In Montreal's Jewish *Quartier*, the boy in me came alive. I had diamonds over my heart. Watching Danielle, I noticed that my eyes were burning, I took a corner of the sweater to wipe the hot salt stinging my cheek. I never needed the hole cut in my windpipe. To help myself, I often thought of that and sang.

"What was it like?" she asked quietly after when she sat by me on the bed. There was no way to explain or to comfort her against the loss of our childhood. I relive those sweatered nights. I hug myself as I cradle the phone, two years and some shy of seventy.

And they thought I would not live through my twelfth summer. Indigo at four years shy of seventy prayed, "Give me back the garment and grail. Give me back Mother ruffling my hair and calling me, 'Red fox! Sly fox!' Father saying, 'Bright Honor! We're bringing you home.' I want the black

---

5   *Etincellante* means sparkling.

scratchy leg warmers, over legs thin as reeds, dangling. Return to me a body boy-long, girl-strong."

January 21-May, 2001 Victoria B.C.

Indigo thought, my father might have asked, *How could one have avoided the suffering of 1951?*

Historically, polio was a disaster of the first hall of the Twentieth Century. Peril and poetry to the child, paralysis was a fact to thousands. It sent whole families into hospitals, paralyzed, some dying. There were no known cures as there are none now, and of course prevention was as yet an untapped godsend. From my hospital bed, I looked on it as a miracle. Perhaps my children would not suffer as I had and would continue to throughout my now rather long life.

How could this level of trauma and torment be avoided?

By communication. Had there been team-work between patient and doctor such as has evolved today, in the early twenty-first century, the child or patient would not have been turned into a victim, made to feel powerless as the central character, or protagonist, here does. The central character is suffering at the hands of the health care system, which had just dealt with the casualties of World War II. Team work even among physicians was in its infancy. The network was more a hierarchy with the king pin the head doctor, the one at top. Ironically, ours was Dr. Deavers, known for his strict crack-the-whip approach of no tears, you'll never get well again but don't whine and complain.

By building a team rather than a hierarchy. The top orthopedic surgeon Dr. Deavers was a man we feared. Under him was our resident, Dr. Pain, most ironically named as if out of *Alice In Wonderland*. Then under him came the nurses, also a hierarchy at whose top stood the head day nurse, then the head night-nurse. Precisely because a system of communication was possible between Mrs. Stanton the head night nurse whom I, the protagonist, Indigo have never forgotten. We children were given some sense that we could take our strength and make it effective.

Teamwork is the core of modern medicine and in the several children's hospitals where I have done volunteer work as a music-therapist, due to my own disability, due to my being in a wheelchair, I have been able to communicate effectively, with caring and humor with children who battle both mental and physical disabilities. With downs syndrome kids, for instance, I have found a special level of emotional openness. It is as though the gate to the unconscious is let down. "I feel—downhearted," said a girl of thirteen one afternoon. With a hydrocephalic boy whose head was so enlarged he had to live in a medieval looking cart, I heard the sweetest version of *Amazing Grace*. Blinded by one of his attacks of hydrocephalus, he said, "Are you there? Knock, knock," and such phrases, which he had learned communicating with nurses. They took the time to consider him as a human being, to interact with him.

"Checks and balances," her father's ghost breathed over Indigo's shoulder.

In 1951, then a doctor, like Dr. Pain, stood at the foot of my bed, reading my chart. He read aloud to a visiting physician, teaching him ostensibly, "Here's a child with two useless limbs."

The next bed might elicit the comment, "Here's one with three useless limbs."

There was no monitoring power to stop such obviously negative and wounding statements before the patient. Today, we have checks and balances. Some of these are learned in courses on patient communication. There are now even literary journals such as the highly literate and superb *Bellevue Literary Review* started by Dr. Danielle Ofri, a Jewish woman doctor who wanted to connect literature with medicine to examine all aspects of doctor-patient relationship, high among them communication. If a doctor, or nurse for that matter, makes a damaging comment, the patient has the right to report it to that person's boss, thus ruling out such behavior, or making it pay a high price tag.

Nurse and therapist negligence. Father, you know that I, Indigo, was left overnight in a wet bed in New York Hospital, Cornell Medical Center, because a nurse was in a bad mood and wanted to punish me for wetting the bed. Again, I was rendered without power and in despair. I rang the button five times that night, it lit up in the nurse's station but the nurse when she arrived said I had buzzed her at the height of some other emergency and since I'd wet the bed she'd leave me in it 'til morning. You, father, reported this, being a doctor himself, and the woman was given notice in the morning. Had I not had this saving connection, I would have suffered further.

Having recently regained bladder control, after it too was paralyzed during the acute phase of polio, I was not going to possibly burst my bladder or strain it further. This is an example of nurse negligence. Was under staffing a problem then as now? And hence over work? If so, this must be addressed.

An example of physiotherapist negligence occurred in Haverstraw, New York State Rehabilitation Center, now euphemized as "The Helen Hayes

Rehabilitation Center" since the great actress lost her only daughter, Mary, overnight to polio. In those days we were given not only the Sister Kenny hot packs which were costly of man power since they were one-on-one: a therapist who had to remain with the patient would heat hot packs and wind the wool around the child's, the patient's limbs after putting them through a wringer. All this was done at the bedside. The purpose was to break the spasm, which afflict the limbs after polio. The limbs are locked. These were supplemented and succeeded by chemical hot packs. I was lain face down over a barrel (literally an old wooden barrel) and a chemical hot pack with coils was placed on my spine. there was a roomful of kids going through the same procedure. The therapist left these packs on which slowly heated. In twenty minutes she was to return, a buzzer serving to remind her. Once she forgot to return and the pack heating up so much I was horrified, I could feel my back beginning to burn and blister. Paralyzed, all I could do was scream for help. When no help came, I nearly threw myself off the barrel wriggling out of the pack.

At night, the master switch was thrown and the ward plunged into darkness. Not only did this create a terrifying cave for sick children but also it made vision cut to a minimum. Before bed, we had nothing to help us sleep: no music, no story hour. The parallel was at the other end of day: dawn. The master switch was thrown too early waking us unnaturally with glare. A bedpan—unheated in those days—was slapped on each kid's bony butt and a roll call of the infant military began calling each child by her last name. I was on a ward for non spastic girls up to age 12. "Bedpan, Strongin! Bedpan, Kowalski!" the cry went.

It was painful and cruel. Directed even then toward links between literature and medicine I, Indigo, had read my polio past. Now it was all laid out for me like the architecture of Christopher Wren's *Saint Paul's*. Or like the figures so elegant and exquisite in *Gray's Anatomy*. The future was to live inside the blueprints, to make the pilgrimage, to go the distance, having memorized in early childhood the rim.

Sobranies

For Deborah

Wicked, sweet-smelling, long and gold-tipped, they were a feature of our early days up north. Then there were tobacco tins, for early morning pipes. Wearing our winter white, we waited for evening to light up. Our winter white came from the Sally Ann in those days. Sweetheart asks, "How's my girl?" and hands me coffee saying, "Here you are, my lady."

Belle, however, is walking in Boston in the cold and catches the phone, "I need my hand," she says. I picture her turtle diving into her navy blue collar.

Our sheer curtains where we are now are slightly weighted at the bottom in order not to blow. Sweetheart had a government job. My old friend Virginia, the brilliant biochemist, commented that any country mainly run by the government could be gray in tone. Someone in the top ministry needs to meet with the others.

One held the gauze up to the sun and saw through to the shine. A bandage wrapping a chest wound also revealed heart. If I am able to see the crystalline through the gray, perhaps it is because the earliest suns I saw as a child in New England were bronze above a Northern River, the Hudson. In winter, it appeared pearl behind satin. I picture a Civil War nurse, one who would never light up a Black Russian (or would she?) Unscrolling bandages in the azure light of the sickroom or the battlefield under artillery of first winter ice, dealing with mortally, the deathly wounded, trying to find a lantern. Blackburn Public Library reading room takes the place of Brick Works.

In my early girlhood, a mousy librarian checked books out in the children's section of the New Rochelle Public Library. The children's library was upstairs. Little tea-colored cards held smaller stiff paper cards on which the due date was stamped. I was breathless before this. The room was the color of dark nicotine. I had a positive feeling toward tobacco then, both my parents sweet-smelling from Old Phillip Morris, its wrappers crinkly and silver, magical for me in the bin. Miss Prinzet however, who invariably had a cold, scared the fear of God into children added to by the fact that she inevitably wore a black pullover, pleated black skirt. In coldest weather she wore a shawl. When Miss Prinzet developed cataracts, she retired, although the operation was not complex. "Like lace over your eye?" I asked.

She nodded. I saw lace. I saw fire burning lace. I saw a waterfall of lace. Her lace was eating up her vision. Fire's appetite is whetted by wind, like the knife-blade by water. It wolfs homes and canyons. Returning to my room, I had a stash of heaven-scented books and determined I'm going to write one of these since they're the best thing in the world, a book when I grow up. Beyond, beyond…

In my memory, swirling, ambient air flows around the wooden horse painted in Sweden, touched up red and blue by our mother half a century ago. Child, I am unwrapping your gauze to find the bone sheen. Fear not. *Je suis medcin*. Maybe only a hospitalized child can dread, as I dreaded, dawn. The window to day, the cover to film, it is unscrolled without mercy. Maybe I saw what the dying see.

I have a friend whose aunt is called Avilene. She is ninety-five. Once a year my friend goes to visit her aunt. "You are my window on life," the aunt tells Norah. Her organdies, Aunt's, are like the window to the frozen Thames when the ice thinned. In a waffle-weave envelope from Britain marked "Royal Mail" I am dropping my old psychologist a copy of my book *Lace-Circled Darkness*. It is this darkness circled with lousy that frames the mousy librarian, and the intense child I am, also with eyeglass, in the silver cold and blue corduroy jumper, on my knees in the New Rochelle Public Library reading. If I look through the gray cobwebby window, so high up as to be almost a clerestory, I can glimpse a pearl sun.

This sun is echoes in my twelfth year, which mirrors so precisely the war years. Hospitalization reflections in correction gives rise to strong stirring of imagination's wings.

Yes, that is a wing pushing through my shoulder blade. During the American Civil War, nurses wrapped stumps of limbs so that they wouldn't bleed. Still, they wept. "Why the huge christening gown?" I ask an Irish Catholic friend, who responds, "I think it must have to do with wealth and station."

Linen and lace was expensive so the longer the gown the more you proclaimed your status! We children, wrapped in Reese jackets, like Civil War soldiers wrapped in casts and bandages, had little wealth or station. This, our carapace, pronounced our vulnerability. Oh time, sweet thief of things.

I am so happy when one hour melts into another hour, it is like pain melting. Not like one taking steps to the scaffold, although if one can hold each day as precious as one's last, how must that be? Hidden behind a glass partition we could see St Paul's dome through the sun of our pain and suffering. At the moment of my treatment the sound of a band drifted in from the street while a parade made its way to some designation, perhaps country church in hushed tones.

After the blade, one wants to be wrapped in blessing garments, not shrouds. Red wool. A doctor's wife, Mother had to be organized but as an artist she instinctively sought beauty and order. She knew disorder breaks the heart. They both did. Yet disorder followed in the wake of their tumultuous love, or rather their love in which each sublimated passion in such a way as to distort their native vigor. Searching for one thing, one finds another. Seeking matrimonial bliss, our mother found *darkest doemstica*. Seeking beauty and paternity, our father discovered schism, division, an echo of his parents discord and ultimate divorce. Seeking to climb the highest mountain my twelfth summer more dexterously than my eleventh, I found paralysis.

Looking just now in the ancestral wood drawer of Miss Maple topped by oval mirror, like our grandmother's, I have discovered our Sobranie Black Russian cigarettes made in England, stamped with Canada. How far back do these rolled black cigarettes with gold tip date? They follow our mother's lung cancer, encapsulated successfully removed so that when the surgeon predicted, "If this woman lives two more years..." and threw up his large hands and raised his eyes. She lived to be ninety-two. Yet the unearthing follows our friend, the jeweler's and his wife the musician's daughter being diagnosed with metastasized lung cancer.

The light spreads in benign fashion through the velvet old oaks out my window, combing them.

We were combed and groomed for emergency, even disaster yet when the red flag came, our hearts beat faster, our pulse soars, our cheeks rouged. We took a deep breath, wanting to leave the dirt behind. This was fortune. Misfortune. I open the box to read, "A fascinating gold-tipped cigarette with finest Russian leaf-they are made from a recipe once exclusively reserved for a Grand Duke at the Court of St. Petersburg. A special cigarette for the connoisseur. A Balkan Sobranie Produce, Sobranie LTD Sobranie House London England."

I came upon Sweetheart's journal of fascinating disclosures and children's stories in sketch form, or so I thought. It was empty. Bluebeard's Castle of Glass. I come upon an article, "Dating English Tins." How well this relates to the knife under the matters, the links inevitable as wave of water to wave of water, thought to thought, love to ardor.

Tin Types

There are three major types of English tobacco tins as well as some minor varieties: The 'knife lid' or 'cutter top' tin style appears to have come into use during World War I (although there may be evidence of late 19th century use) and was generally used through the 1960s. This tin type has two tops, a disposable metal inner top used to create an airtight seal and a loose metal outer top. The inner top is a thin metal sheet, which effects an air seal until the initial opening of the tin. The outer top is used to initially open the tin by cutting away the inner top (the inner top being then disposed of) and then used to loosely cover the opened tin. There is a cutting point on the inside of outer top near the edge that comes in one of two styles 'fixed' and 'moveable'.

Nonetheless cancer can writhe in blue smoke out of the box or tin. We once had a round tin. It bore the weight of our passion, for each other, for the exotic and the Bohemian.

My early love for my mother and father is linked to the image and scent of their smoking rich tobacco blends. I think of war English blends. Smoking went with the heroine.

The 'coin twist' tin, which is still used today, appears to have been introduced in the 1940's following World War II and by the '70s became the predominant tin style. Some early 'coin twists' dating to no later then the early 1950's had rubber gaskets that extended past the outer lip of the top or rubber stoppers that plugged a hole in the bottom of the tin.

By a leap of imagination which I hope contains a synapse, I move from these words to the image of our father bending over slides under the microscope in his early pioneering studies on vision and its relation to human emotion. Earlier, he had studied stimulus and caffeine in Coca-Cola.

Stimulus: that is what I craved most as a child flat on my back, immobilized. The light provided stimulus, the sun swirling across sky like a bead of mercury round a tilted bowl cupped in the hands, or that drop of brandy in the sniffer, or the one kernel of precious gold in the wooden bowl. I think too of the finger making a chime round the glass, proving it genuine crystal, which draws me back to that strip of gray-white cellophane, pale as bone, I hold up to the sun and through which I see pearl light like that of Vermeer's *Girl with the Pearl Earring* in the window in Holland: contemplative, complex as lace, her expression bespeaking her emotions.

But what are those emotions? Is it merely Bluebeard's Castle of which she dreams, which she protects with her nubile body like child in womb? A thing, a miracle perhaps, she has not yet known despite assignations with the candle maker's son, sixteen, Hans.

I have looked up Fewterer: *A keeper of greyhounds. Also in a wider sense, an attendant. Also with defining word prefixed; as fox-, yeoman-fewterer.*

○

It is almost my getting out time. I have and am no fewtere. Rather, I peel back layer after layer of memory like mica until the sheets themselves are radiant as the very finest tulip-tissue layers of glass. Layers of a bridal gown billow on a baby in late-morning sun. The deliciousness and mystery of enclosure magnetizes me. I read up on Dunhill Tined Tobacco and recall my first lesbian love, smoking. There are Campaign Mixture tins and there are Standard Mixtures. Undone with coin-twist or knife they stand, sturdy as the British Empire. I observe that there is a Dunhill's Royal Yacht brand and think of jeweler and musician's daughter and peeling back layers of cancer, inevitably the pathologist's, the clinician's daughter. So honored or dishonored. The warrant to one type Dunhill, a favorite of Edward, Prince of Wales, named in his honor in 1921, was removed with the abdication of the Prince of Wales who too had a label. Look! Here stands "My Mixture" something Mother Marcelle might have used to light the taper of magic on a sleety winter day like those over the frozen Thames. It has a sweet nostalgic pong. There is an Early Morning Pipe mixture and Dunhill's Three Year, in addition to The Aperitif. I would lay all my life before me in such delectable tins bearing the authentic signature of Alfred Dunhill. Let' send with Nightcap mixture. Sweetheart and I, place us back on Cook street, would be smoking at noon the golden table in front of the window overlooking the bus shelter which rattled and hung with a blue table cloth for drape. A bright shiny gold tone metal with pronounced roll at lower lip it would enhance the décor of our home, and help define it.

Bitterroot

She flew in an old World War II plane with minimal comfort, wrapped in an army blanket. Flew for the yearly visit to her sister, Alma, who was performing in the little mountain town of Telluride, Colorado. Physiology is destiny, she thought, being wheeled into the forklift, the bumped off the ramp.

"Sarne! Welcome," her sister and brother-in-law hugged her and drove her home to the cabin. It had three steps and too narrow a bath door for the chair to fit through.

Sarne decided, undressing to rest for evening, folk make both too much and yet too little of the blind and the lame living in a private, intensely heightened universe. She yanked the drapes, whose pull she couldn't reach, to block out the blinding Colorado sun in August at four in the afternoon. This was the highest state. This was their high point of the year, Alma's and Sarne's. Their reunion. It took place wherever Mike and Alma were teaching for summertime; one of the large international festivals. Not far from Roaring Fork Junction and South Original Street. Like Aspen, it was of course, a ski resort, a winter wonderland half the year, this early mill and mining town. She felt, nonetheless, a strong sense of fortune having passed her by as she lay down.

Rising, she yanked open the green rigged up drape. The sun was still strong. There was Alma coming home, a sack of laundry thrown across her back. She didn't like admitting that she envied Alma this mobility. The young, the strength, married, of having a lover, and a sack of laundry to do every other day, but above all the youth and strength to sling it over your back. White in the late day, a contrast to our swarthy complexion.

Lucky Alma.

Sarne kept seeing that large-boned figure, Lee, rise among the flames these long evenings she spent alone in Colorado, in the cabin, while Alma and Michael were off rehearsing.

She would see Lee at random moments, stocky build super-imposed on slender Semitic features of Alma.

After supper out at the Charbroil House, in the too-red heat of the Rocky Mountain setting sun, she, Sarne, saw earth as a slag heap. With Alma, she saw the towns of their lives as a succession of bricked-in linen-mills, boarded-up wells; slatted furnaces in industrial New England towns.

Elegy rang bell-clear.

Why?

Had either woman some blind spot toward the feelings of her sister? Maybe it was that moment in a woman's life when she realizes, sharply as though a mine bell were rung, sat she'd have to accustom herself to the idea of a life either with, or without marriage.

At any rate, Sarne felt distant from Alma during this time and the reverberations of this twilight bell, its muted clang through a scarlet sunset, filled the entire visit.

Even the dog. His head resembled a burst basketball, zigzag white wool everywhere sproinging. His eyes were indiscernible raged grey-white strings. He looked dirty. His nose was black sponge. Dirty and vulnerable. Left alone, like Sarne, long hours, he was nervous, high-strung and ravenous when they came home and barked at any footfall, which meant often. Torn between baying and wagging his tail.

"No barking! No barking!" Sarne scolded over and over but to no avail.

Then Skeezicks!, she'd shout and throw the dish towel at him at which he'd only play with, starved for fun as he was, and shake it in his snout. They were akin.

Equally relieved when Alma and Mike came home.

Sarne had a series of bad afternoons with the dog. First a female kept coming round, then once he wandered off and she though she'd lost him. Another afternoon he got himself entangled in the telephone, when she went to answer it, tangling it further in a wheel of the chair. The dog was asthmatic. That was another thing about him, old basketball head.

Afternoons were her low time anyhow. One afternoon, Alma brought Sarne Professor Edmon's Rose-Water & Glycerin.

She also brought a postcard from Lee. "Kiddo, How are you feeling? Is it great to be among kin again? Our voice sounds strong. They love you a lot. Lee." The card was in color and showed a swatch of the Oregon Trail.

They love me, Sarne thought, yet Lee was the one she'd wanted to kiss her that night by the ocean. She longed for Lee's strong practical nature and recalled it was Lee who told her, "You shouldn't be nailed twice: polio then me."

Lee would be down the coast she realized, bottle-tipping. Lee was one with whom you could sit still and almost hear the earth turn.

Sarne plunged into the old foggy-blue leather chair evenings, but desisted smoking. Sarne stared down the long thin hall where hooks for ski jackets were driven into the wall. Squinting, she could observe bars of stained glass in the front door, red, gold, purple and green blurred like old mackinaws turned to wax candles melting.

Sarne wrote a postcard to an old college chum.

Maggie: I'm visiting my sister and husband here in the Colorado mountains. It's bread and nails. Are you out there Maggie? Still in New York publishing? We had a strange connection, a dream phone conversation last night. Write. Sarne.

She plunged deeper and deeper into the leather, smoked from time to time when Skeezicks was out back in the yard barking. She practiced dialing the 10 numbers for Maggie's but never even got to raising the phone from its hopper to progress to the dial tone.

The next afternoon the Doberman pup upstairs broke in. She and Skeez went on a rampage, overturning garbage, strewing it about the living room. His eyes snapped like black marbles in his white head. Sarne was powerless to control them. She drew the drapes but he was bright, nosing his soft snout through them. He rolled his butcher knucklebone clotted with blood and gristle. He dragged and shoved these bones until they split into two, and one piece of bone hung from the other.

"Dog drives me nuts," she complained to Alma.

But Sarne never spoke of the true fox in her breast.

Alma may have had hints, but did she know for a fact that Sarne had loved a woman? Yes, Jan too, a prince of a man. She wanted to bring up Lee but didn't know how. They took a few walks to the Glory Hole Park, they ate at The Shaft, went to bed early when they were rehearsing.

Sarne dreamed of coke-ovens, bricked in linen mills as she fell into restless slumber.

She missed real coffee, mornings. Coffee strong enough to stand on its own. Alma and Jan didn't count on mail as Sarne did, as a writer. This was a further letdown, an alienation. They fetched it at the real estate P.O. Box in the town of Telluride.

Mail was the very leaven of life.

I'm going to tell them a white lie, she decided, that I must leave soon to plan autumn syllabus for a new course I'm teaching. They'll understand.

She resolved this each afternoon as the lonely hour of four tolled in, like a bell. Then lightened up in the evening. "The biggest labor of life is to become patient with each other," she'd scrawled to herself on the side of a poem. Days were trees in a dark forest, a knot, to her mind.

But reading way past midnight, Sarne was able to recapture some of the haven of closeness she'd felt with Alma when they were girls under Jo-Jo's roof. At isolated moments, she had an epiphany. The white light would shine when she scrubbed Alma's kitchen counters down or enjoyed lamplight flickering upon walls of the redwood cabin. She felt she was the unmoving stone at the center of the whole scene however.

The animal tied down by a silver chain now to the Edison, he became so rambunctious one afternoon. If she cracked the front door for a breath of air, he got loose.

When the two came home tired, trudging in the cabin door, their instruments in tow, she brewed a pot of hot tea for them.

"Was Rags good?"

"Skeezicks?"

"Yes."

"Yes. Old burst-basketball head and me, he's fine." She laughed. How could she tell them the hard things?

"Want me to wheel you round front to see the mountains?" asked Alma. "Never seen so many stars."

No, she wanted to answer, I don't want you to wheel me round, I want to run around like you and see the stars. Alma was four years younger. Could she remember those last steps Sarne had taken that unearthly night, that eerie nightfall, through the haze of exhaustion and pain? The willpower it took to summon up strength to take those steps when the virus was already attacking her spine?

Instead, she circled her sister and said, "You're worn, Alma, get some sack." Her sister, slender at twenty-five, wore red lisle knees-stockings she'd bought on tour in London, medium-heeled shoes, and had purple rings under her eyes. Still getting over jet jag, only five days. Sarne brushed back the fragrant cloud of dark hair from Alma's cheek, and kissed it. Alma had a voice to go with her name, gentle as a dove.

"What was I like when I could walk?"

"You couldn't be contained."

Alma laid her strong, violists' hand on Sarne's shoulder. She worked out the knots. It reweaves the bond between them, the kindness. It took the tiredness from her arms.

The next morning, they woke to one of those sudden mountain thunder storms. Jan drove Sarne to the Pitkin County Library with a map of Pathfinder on the wall. She felt like a dark horse in the library. Under the stuffed town on the wall, and round wood wall clock. Three o'clock. Rain. Small boys belly-to-belly on the floor at the head of the stairs, poking fingers through. "Chitty Chitty Bang Bang," cries one in yellow oilskin slicker. One boy has hiccups, which echo through the quiet building. The placid, peasant voice of the reader drones behind him. Story hour for younger children.

Sarne leafed through a history of the sawed-off shotgun in Colorado.

"Your soul is simon-pure," she scrawled on the back of an envelope.

She thought of Lee.

Driving home, they encountered the second half of the electrical storm. The yellow traffic light on Third Street was blowing back and forth. Chilled, she took a warm bath and headed into bed early after a cup of Lipton Instant.

○

"I know thou hast felt thyself vulnerable from the first," she always drifted into the Quaker *thee* and *thou* when she addressed Lee in a dream, as though they'd been cast back into an earlier time. "I cannot study thee closely enough to make myself as strong as I seek to become. I know you have suffered by this calm, this renunciation. Have learned to master the world—as Emily did—by renouncing it. I do not mean to break through, Lee-Lo.

"Maybe it's a religious war that's occurring between us," she whispered to Lee at her elbow in the second dream. "Your restraint, my openness, at loggerheads. A religious war, Imagine! In the Twentieth Century."

But there's no comment from Lee in her Irish cardigan and trench coat over.

It was now that Sarne began haunting Pitkin County Library and decided she had a reason to stay on.

When she returned, next afternoon, the librarian laid her hand on her shoulder, and wore hiking boots. A two-day summer book sale was on to get ready for autumns. Lots of beer-cartons stood around with motley colored books in them.

Maybe it is a religious war, she went on writing in her mind. Half closing her eyes, Sarne folded the book and felt three-year-olds brush up against her knees. She was a child again, a daughter of time, running her hands along butterscotch, scarred wood, cracking her knuckles, speaking to God about various things.

Then the apparition occurred for the second time!

They were two horses in a field of wildflowers, she and Lee, wild fillies this time. She, who moved in back of her chair in that pea-colored raincoat to the middle of the calf, had turned into a sorrel filly. The white shirt collar turned up about her ears was a diamond, for hair not speckled silver but sandy.

All Lee's reflexes were good. So were the filly's.

Her combination of realism and affection made her prompt.

"Be a mild Emily. The fire will come out in your writing."

"Do you need any help?" It was the soft-spoken, buck-toothed smile of the librarian. Raking the dark of that face for token of affection, Sarne turned round. A long history of afternoons of visiting libraries and kin: smoldering boredom and grief.

She could read the face of the librarian.

"No, thank you," embarrassed she bent her head studying the words:

"This book was manufactured under wartime conditions."

Rags. Skeeziks. Her mind flashed back to the dog. Then like a movie camera panning out, swung round the room. She'd no longer felt cruel toward the mutt these past few days. She'd seen him bathed, the hound come out like a sheath of white wool. Alma bought him a valise tag. She even began to enjoy a midday yogurt break with him. In the library, every afternoon, she wrote. Every once in a while applause would thunder out from the sunken children's section, a sound like bacon quickly being fried or doughnuts bubbling.

One remembers from childhood being dragged to the edge of the town, seeing a pile of tires being burned in a refuse lot. One remembers, she does, that it is behind the gasworks that horrors breed...

"Closing time," the librarian says, "It's you and I alone." She looks up and smiles.

Alma was late at a rehearsal so Jan picked her up. Then the close-call came.

There was a bark of brakes, they stopped just in time to avoid hitting Rags. Jan leapt out of the car, and gathered his dog up. His eyes bore the glassy stare of the dying, despite little blood.

The vet said he'd be ok, but he'd keep Skeezicks-Rags in a week for observation. He might have internal bleeding. The mirage, the ghost of him floated in and out of their cabin at one hundred years old all that week.

Alabama Light & Power Co

At odd times.

Bowing their heads over prayer at breakfast, the only grace they said.

Or earlier morning, in fog.

When they bent to pile fresh laundry.

Sarne would watch Alma coming home. Along Roaring Fork Junction, down South Original in coppery evening, glad she'd stayed on. There was the writing now, and the library each afternoon, the apparitions of Lee, and even the librarian. Alma, her two bags of wash, bags of gold, and bags of feathers. Yoked in matrimony, even she became handsome to Sarne this week Rag's life lay in the balance. Alma, younger sister, sang Jewish folk songs to the guitar accompaniment of Jan some evenings while Sarne became aware of a violence that had been flowing like blood through her subsiding. It is a rhythm of life, she knows, table turning. Life's not a level playing field, she understood. Alma more than ever would circle her arms, though brief, about her older sister as if she could quell the curses rising in the woman, circling inside her like a dog chasing its tail, a planet chasing its orbits.

Sarne bought Alma a blue suede belt in town. The transparent mountain air had cleared her head. Movement was euphoric. She had one heart-to-heart with Alma, saying, "I think Jo-Jo and I have been cruel to one another sometimes, but it's due to frustration."

She went into crystal night. She could feel the buildings clearly as one could the stilled mines. Ski-cars would soon be readied to lift and descend again, in winter. She felt quickened by the presence of skiers. What was out of joint in her was now in.

The mirage of Lee had bent above her in Pitkin County Library like glowing coals that early evening. Blown upon, she'd come alive. I know, decided Sarne, something about the appearance of the celestial stag now.

She dreamed they were back on the coast, before Sarne flew to the state beneath Colorado. Lee had the kiwi for surprise.

"I'll leave you soon," Lee had said. Let you get some rest."

But first she'd cracked the second kiwi open in Sarne's empty apartment. Red-hot, faithful as rain.

"Come. It's rough outside, and drab, but smooth within."

Their last evening was kingfisher blue.

The next afternoon, "I'll leave you soon." Sarne turned to face Alma.

They'd had an early fish dinner for which Sarne had tossed on an old ratty fur coat Jo-Jo had thrown her way—a parting shot, fur in July—when she'd left the coast to fly to the desert. Sarne had brought it to the high mountains, her thinness still drawing the chill in. Mulling over her article "Psychological Rag-Time," she realized things become, as a rule, frantic, gay after war. She had a flashback wearing the coat. In this coat, cut out of the flaming twenties—from which Lee took in Sarne's image with great mirth—the two women had gone along the boardwalk. The two sisters, Alma and Sarne, pushed along, reminiscent of Lee and Sarne, but to the creek at South Original, not far from Roaring Fork Junction.

Alma bent down to brush the sandy blonde hair out of Sarne's eye and kissed her good night at the door to her room, just the way Lee had after they'd laughed at finding parking meters the exact color of Lee's toenails which flashed in open-sands.

Hung over, Lee had turned up late to see Sarne off at the airport.

"Don't call me any more." Sarne had said to Lee at the airport.

But to Alma, no words.

"Here," she'd shoved the bunch of wildflowers bought on impulse toward her sister, who looked, for all worlds, like a survivor of one of the camps, as well as of that endless war. I am interested in what survives, rubbings... Lee was a spectacle, one turned eyes toward her. Alma was a commanding presence, an artist, and a dancer. The bitterroot had been cracked open and the light flowed like liquid fire.

Her heart roped under her windbreaker when she woke at night to take a smoke on the terrace. She tried not to waken the dog. She felt the curve from abdomen to thigh. She longed for Lee. Her breasts like small firm oranges, like Christopher Wren's St. Paul's dome, but in duplicate, two of them. And now, Lee and I, we are surrendered: where we were two, only one.

Twilight, Heart-Side

If we are in our twilight, morning is far behind, glistens, shining at the far end of the time telescope. But heart aside I keep Anyushka, Sweetheart, all the others for arterial power. Artemis. Anyushka wasn't playing with a full deck, she wrote. She was playing with ten decks.

Mad for hugging, Sweetheart comes home in long black raincoat more gorgeous than ever after fourteen houses away from home. I have made up my mind not to begin with what a long day you've had, trooper!

She sits on the bed her raincoat on. "We had three kinds of salad for the buffet on the spirit of Vancouver ferry. Having missed the five o'clock sailing, we lucked in. The entrees were sliced white meat turkey or dark if one preferred, roast beef with lean, and baked salmon with a Hollandaise sauce. Not only that, Indigo, but there were three types of desert. I made the mistake of not taking two pieces of the lemon chiffon square."

"Well done," I smile.

This is a marathon even for Belle whom I see passing phones on the way to the stage from dressing room, tensing, being told she is wanted. Given a kiss before stage.

Why did I walk back and back to her on my last trained walking? It was the summer she was seven and I was eleven. I rode ahead of her in the train, which went forward in the night of course but seemed to go backward because driven, with a compulsion not unknown to me, I returned and returned to plant a kiss on my little sister's cheek. I also checked my own image out as if locking it for all time in my thin pocket mirror I kept on the side of my jeans. I was changing: gray eyes were more green, stony luminous and opaque. My Strongin heart-shaped face was becoming longer. The words "keep good care of me" were drawing me, keeping us both no doubt company.

This was true of my brother-and-law and Belle, with a touch that's tender as a kiss and just as dangerous. Just how this royal couple gets along on stage, given their stylistic differences, is a mystery that will be answered in October

We perceive faces extremely quickly, especially fearful eyes where more of the white shows. We are programmed to recognize fear in another's face. Look out! There's a scared person over there. I better be scared too. A neutral and happy face does not do this. Our faces are a microcosm of our macrocosm.

○

If we are in twilight, night is to follow. Sweetheart is overtired, radiant though she may have appeared. Mad for hugging today, I do not suggest hats. But she is up making good smells waft down the hall form the kitchen to where I write. I already scent burned toast crumbs, multi-grain, and coffee. O sweet strong Scot. Never carrying any weight, then I was translucent when most ill. Now the tables are not turned, but all struggles being power struggles, we bat like a Punch and Judy in the Park who love each other yet can be blown to smithereens.

Smithereens. What say my friend from UK?

If the morning we have most éclat, in the evening we have the quiet smile. Those who suffer most laugh most. Those who suffer least are most dour, sullen. How can one page eternity? I flashback to my last chapter. If I keep running back hugging and hugging Belle, wasn't it because with a brush of ivory we are always painting in for a last time, the faces of our beloveds? We are always saying a last goodbye—I still am to Rosaleen—on the platform of time?

Yes, this blue planet is studded with platforms of time, in various countries where heart-side we hold twilight, and then death and are voicing in our most eloquent Hamlet soliloquy a farewell to time.

"We are cloned!!!" writes Kathleen-Rose, with whom I am in the doghouse.

In the Sweetheart nightie photo, I noted we have the same kitchen cupboards

○

Will you forgive me, darlings if I put you in a shared room? New Zealander with a map of Ireland written all over her lovely, lilting face. Scotswoman with tender, fierce disposition. Face set for the long haul. Hockey at night, lit by lights, which make the glow on the snow blinding. Zambonis? No, I shall not be forgiven so I will lift the little cups for their cupboards and recall sweetheart's language about the saucers and cups she found for her parents.

Sweetheart always mellows things, very English, more Canadian? "Not a problem. No fright. No worries. I'll just gently slope by, swing by your house."

As a home maker, she won the hearts of Mrs. Klamaroth who liked beef broth, Mrs. Woolsey who dripped urine (she padded around calm as an English rose yet had her thorn). Mrs. Nielsen gave her the terra-cotta clay baker, which we have roasted our Thanksgiving turkey leg in for years. Yes, here in Canada life is more from the U.K. All the English pigeons have come home to roost, to live, like natty Rosaleen, thirty, on two pensions not to replace the area railing. Being British, we inherit war rags and digs. It is all a bit more beloved for being downtrodden. But Jewish princess, Mama Marcelle says, "I see you trying, trying to please her and I feel so sorry for you I could cry," but Sweetheart showed the thorns on her rose when she came home.

We hit the bottle.

Self-inflicted wounds wrecked a score of our mornings. Generally it would burn off by noon. Nonetheless, I played piano at hospitals for mentally and spiritually challenged children. After all, I'd been one. A five-year-old's height, or the height of a Saint Bernard, I was one of them.

By evening, the gold of Jack Daniels, or the silver of Beefeaters Gin gleamed, Mecca, a mirage once again and the lovely glasses we'd bought at the Twice-Around on Antique Row, Fort, were tenderly lifted down. "Uh oh," Sweetheart said one night, "fatty oily fingerprints. We'll retire this glass."

And hard those first years. I was married to her but I was also married to gin.

Bottle-tipping, it's no exaggeration to say, went with smoking like a chimney. But we puffed only the dragon-lady's best, child dragon and I only Sobranies Black Russian.

"Look, I bought you a circular canister of them!" Sweetheart beamed, thin as a rail. She'd procured a round tin of Black Russians to fill our railroad flat. With the hardwood floors and north light, bus shelter rattling outside all day and night, it filled with the fragrance sweet as wood fire burning had been back in our desert home.

"Do you like it?" I asked Mother Marcelle. We had a half-table, golden pond, from IKEA we fastened in the window overlooking the rattling bus shelter. We named everything. Wing is our rose armchair in which Sweetheart curls like a child and reads for hours. In which I proof my books. The half table? Moon. We lit candles at it. We hung an old table cloth, Swedish, cobalt blue and white embroidery, in the bedroom window for curtains and lined the window with stained glass, our cathedral, old Mateus jars.

"It's darling," she said, "but it depresses me."

She knew after all that one day I would be an heiress, if a modest one. She saw me as the girl who had walked up and down Park Avenue, hands thrust in a bunny fur muff, a cross-eyed Jewish child of the forties with mud-blond hair. Indigo, the mud drab bird. "Shiksa," she'd say, "they'll take you for one."

I shook my head. I blinked. Belle blinked. Mother Marcelle seeing Sweetheart and me in this railroad flat.

Sweetheart having taken a job in Vancouver announced, "She's a Lesbian. You're not one, are you?" And followed it by, "She'll leave you."

After mother's death, her diary sketchbook came into my hands which was appropriately named because she only sketched her grief. Belle always gives too much of herself to others.

Once I cried in front of Sweetheart. Mother said, "Tears in front of a Gentile." She puts others first. Indigo has the intellectual and poetic gifts. That tall Canadian girl has taken my place. I saw her enter in Indigo's life and I was dumped."

But, a closet Lesbian whom my father said "is not a Lesbian but has Lesbian tendencies," Mother saw that Jeannot back in Berkeley was wrong for me. "You're barking up the wrong tree with that woman. She'll drive herself off a cliff one of these days."

Jeannot was a closet case too and a functional alcoholic. I loved her Falstaffian energies. She lived in the morning of her life teaching at a little girl's school in the placid foothills of Berkeley but retaining the zing of her dawn energy, her zest for living.

Twice-alive she was like the delicate, disturbed Anyushaka, the radiant maternal Kathleen-Rose. I do get K Rose's Irish but then I'm a Jew. We are both tribes of pariahs, Ishmaels. "We did not wear skirts and my mother excelled at math, not baking. We wore kilts," writes the mock-outraged K Rose from across the ocean. Good job for us two; she is across the pond this dawn.

What were those teacups like?

What was Belle like when her daughter was a burner? She used her father's Gillette's, I imagine. Sometimes twenty slashes on her ballerina's belly. I did not have to inflict my wounds. Life did that, but my early mysticism was the rehearsal. "I scrubbed and scrubbed the room down," she told me, "and painted the little chair at her desk her favorite color, burgundy."

See red, a trail of blood followed the daughter until she learned to put menstrual blood to better use, that of desire.

○

Listen, sister, *Zelo Green At the Sewing Machine* is playing. Low-keyed, dark-voiced Sweetheart and I are choosing upholstery for our barrel chair. "I could drawl you a sketch," she told Chirstable, the upholstery chef. Oops I mean the blustery woman who is upholstery tailor in our neighborhood, the sheltered Oak Bay.

Imagine what concoctions an upholstery chef might whip up? Baked Alaska hassocks, armchairs with cherry tussocks and pom-poms. A den of iniquity quickly spring to mind. Hot flash pink.

Colin Courtesy Phones. A real name? Yes, the upholsterer's sidekick. Meanwhile, here's to my mid day if twilight is the emotional and spiritual state we are in. Nyushka has written me about underwear in response to my store. It is not all lightweight. I used to fantasize a youth in Europe between the wars. I was a member of your family, inspired. I had trouble with underwear too. In second grade—the object of other kids' persecution since nursery school, some classmates cornered me on the dirt playground, yanked off my panties and an appointed emissary went to the principal's office reporting that Anyushka Moss was prancing around the playground showing her behind. I tried naturally to defend myself to the principal. She didn't believe me. Thank God she didn't call that bitch, my mother, named after Dante! Belle."

Anyushka goes on to tell me of Belle, Viking out of Wagner, visiting, inviting Anya and two friends to her hotel room, thinking herself so beautiful she proceeded to strip down to her girdle."

I recall Belle running around corners, eyes on top of a girdle at age two.

When Anyuskha's mother showed off, Anya and girlfriends tried to not notice. Marcelle, Anya notes, "had good reason for going without underwear, but good grief, Belle was in her fifties. It was very, very strange. She was feeling competitive I'll bet with three younger women."

She hated Austen Riggs which she refers to as the head factory. I was flat-chested. "Lucky you," wrote Anya, who developed early and whose mother barked and snarled, "I hope you won't end up top-heavy like Will's mother."

Like my beloved, and also distrusted, Rosaleen Anya has logorrhea and fears getting the chatty-Cathies. She once lost a job to it. Her favorite colors are pink, gold and burgundy. She sees I am keeping good care of everyone and that whereas our daddy said, "Thank god for Sweetheart," everybody reaches out to me for a pillar strength, I who cannot walk can fly.

○

"I don't tell the truth. I tell what *ought* to be the truth, and if that is sinful, let me damned for it!" Anya quotes Blanche du Bois.

Listen Sweetheart and Kathleen-Rose who damn me.

Or do you rather side with me pinned by love and imagination to my side at night like Icarus' wings which will melt from the sun?

Sweetheart flits about nude. Unlike Belle she is a true beauty: long waist, Ingress body, the gold untouched within. "Remember the Robert Lewis exhibition," she points at me like taking a photograph of an old oak, emerging like gold tapestry of fog. So let my words, Kathleen. "Go! Put on something," I admonish. "I must phone the upholstery chef." We both laugh. "You look beautiful in anything and I look beautiful in nothing."

She disappears. As the Catholic woman said the other day, "Before making music, I must disappear." Thank God she didn't say, "I must go to the little girls' room."

"True, I am mother-father to Sweetheart, was to Belle, cold hands," Rosaleen said at goodbye at our first meeting, adding, "I can't return your gift. I am not rich. I am very poor."

Like storybook tea Mad Hatters, I have given Sweetheart a happy childhood. After all, her mother went to Braxton, a haughty girls' school in Toronto, a boarding school, mainly because of some dimly-recalled dental work that had to be done in her sixteenth winter. Sweetheart has comfortingly dim memories of childhood envelope din a crème-swirl where as mine stand out: Jewish, judgment, vivid as the thorns on Christ's crown.

No, Anyushka, I have no direct memory of the Magdalene bakers from Rosaleen. Isn't childhood in a ward with steam burning one like salt, yes I might have been a salt abortion, burned, scarred who lived—isn't that enough to transport one visually into the Magdalene laundries with children turned into slaves?

"It's like fitting a person," I tell Sweetheart, "measuring our little barrel chair. What would you call the color we favor?"

I wait for the answer. It will sound like whipped cream on cupcakes, I have the sense. The other night suddenly sweetheart craved whipped cream for her cocoa.

"Color? And shall we consider piping"

I reread words of Anya's waiting for Sweetheart to come in with the color check. "I went into the church today and it was no more filled with the spirit than this room. I used to get a feeling of spirituality when I'd visit the Duomo in Florence, but no more than when I'd go by myself and meditate in Savonarola's cell, gazing at his rouse and his hair shirt."

"I'd call it brick. The corduroy will make a soft seat for you."

I resist saying you have the padding. I phone Christable Upholstery, all the time a laugh bubbling in my throat like that in the throat of a quail.

"We would like the Andara, designer is Roy, # 07."

It will happen because Sweetheart wrote it all down. Rolling the word Andara, I hear music, see Kathleen-Roses two husbands, her three children extravagantly beautiful and flick that swatch off like a light when one leaves a room.

It is now nightfall. The room is bathed in dark cream. "Ok," writes Anya, "so the guards might have thought she's weird but she's a contribution to the city's economy."

Economy. We children were threatened. "Yer bed'l run out if yer gone more than forty-eight."

The forty eight were hours. The speech, yes mirrored the speech of a London street urchin who pointed at the stars and said, "Look at all them bedbugs!"

I'm looking.

Looking steadily, Anya and K Rose, loving you both so much I can taste it. You will take offense? My mysticism. Marcelle would have wanted a hairless face. Anya writes, "Without electrolysis I'd look like Abraham Lincoln. Life is a comedy to the one who thinks, a tragedy to the one who feels."

She is home. Sweetheart. Heartside. Exhausted. Sweetheart with her chocolate cocoa moustache, or her down one of real hair. New York is my brown shawl, brownstones, I wrap about my shoulders to keep warm these October winter-coming-in nights. Beyond, in that twilight of the aging before night comes. I will have no more blows to my face if I can possibly avoid it, but mother-father to sweetheart and you, Belle.

Belle, so often I came home and Marcelle wrung every last drop of pity form me like blood from the chicken's neck, "The baby is coming down with something."

"Again?" I asked. I was the only one who ever came down with anything. We are all London urchins, we all wear kilts, we all have coal-smudged faces, we all point up at the stars and "look at them bedbugs."

I am afraid the marble floor must rise to meet my face as inevitably as dark must ultimately rise like waters to swirl black gowns around us all. It is important to state that it was in the iron-lung little round mirror that the newly-paralyzed woman saw her wedding hat, supposedly, reflected in. I may have missed that my first time round, women. Aren't all my tales addressed to women? My musings. My muse.

The Horse Would Tell It Differently

Stallion Sweater: Palomino Pullover

Tell your children, "You are the strength," she said. "Surviving is hard work."

Two years shy of seventy, Keesia is a woman whose voice directed me to her as a survivor of the Blitz in London: I myself was a survivor of a state hospital much like a concentration camp for children. After polio I learned surviving was the hardest work. Work too is a four-letter word. I'd learned to smoke like pile driver in the hospital stairwell at age twelve. I was no girl on a poster, but sat straight in my wheelchair as a jockey on a horse.

She, a Spartan, who wore the Jewish star I gave her because she said she was "spiritually a Jew," who'd been seven when the dark lashed out and descended over the sky of London. The docks were ignited by bombs, by incendiaries and became infernos, hell-holes which burned day and night and day again like Dante's inferno the conflagration.

I, twelve, was brought home half the weight I was before, but twice the fighter. "Indigo, don't put your boxing gloves up on the shelf," Mother Marcelle commanded. This was the game I was playing from now on, the if you can't make it, fake it, game, I the girl mistaken for a boy, so flat-chested at twenty, I the girl with the coke-bottle green eyes a bit asymmetrical whom people compared to a Modigliani, whom people took for a speed freak I was so thin. A silhouette, I was in it for the kill the relentlessly, tough roulette of life. Father said the night he carried me into my old wooden wheelchair to put in his car, "We're bringing bright Honor home."

Honor was his nickname for me.

At fifty, and at sixty, the woman Keesia could still wake, sensing in her eyes the smoke, which billowed scorching. Brought over on the boat from Ireland at a tender eight months, Keesia always considered herself Irish, a passionate Anglo-Irish woman whose husband had drunk their paychecks; who more than once came home in clothes she did not recognize; who, even when he gave up the bottle, would die a dry drunk. Keesia, sure of what was to be valued in life—Kees shared this with me, Toscin-Manon.

Infantile paralysis, the dread of our childhood, had struck me. Violent as rape, the virus had scoured my central nervous system, attacked the myelin sheath of my spine—taken my legs away but left me song to sing. For Keesia, the Blitz, had taught early the inestimable worth of life: what it meant to hear bombers stop above, to die mentally, with that physical anguish, many times before, without the real death. A heart-stopper after which—curtains! Keesia says her younger sister, Maggie "rises easily," I thought, well if Maggie's anger fuses out, what about Keesia?

Half-hazel, half-violet eyes. Keesia looked worn today to me, though when she laughed, I could see bluegrass bending in those smoky eyes. Was she smoking too much again? Was her paralyzed left shoulder heavy? Isn't most criticism pointing our finger at the mirror? The horse, of course, might tell it differently, the horse whose back is nearly broken carrying the rider through oatmeal-drab afternoons and blindingly black midnights.

"It's Kathleen," she smiled, miming tipping the bottle into her mouth, "a bender. Will she never learn she's her own worst enemy? May she marry a ghost and bear him a kitten! She doesn't drink like you and me, spasmodically."

Keesia was the original Mrs. Malaprop, choosing the approximate wrong word with such charm it shone. Her daughter's husband had to learn that "*Dissipating* his emotions would only enrich him." Her degree from The London School of Economics was something she prided herself on like her Irish birth.

She repeated, "If they get the message from you, they are the strength, they will go through life armed."

One of her two kids had died at seventeen, which is why she had a hole in her heart. She lived in Shock City. Ever since, she'd been offering her services to whoever she perceived needed them. If there was a bus strike, she'd pick up women waiting for a bus. "There's no point in going round with an empty car," she down played it. Finding someone parked on the curb with a battery that needed charging , she'd hop out, "I've got jump cables. What's the use drivin' around with them not usin' them?"

"Where did you get this sense of rescuing people?"

"I never had a childhood. Up to age six perhaps I did. But once we were in the midst of war, Mummy made sure I was guardian for the five little ones. I still think I can patch up the world, the way I did for my little brothers and sisters. But I've got a hole in my heart big as a crater on the moon."

I began recalling the map of the wards where I'd lost the last part of what would have been my childhood.

"Facially," she changed the subject which was like the sun coming out, "in the bones of your face, you're one of the few who remains young."

"Am I?" But emotionally I am roaming the wards for a tin cup, a lost bunny with a torn ear and a tea-colored stain where his mouth should have been.

I saw her in the photograph with the wide-brimmed hat when she was twenty-five.

"I don't like myself in age. I look in the mirror and think—my God, what's happened? If I compare what the glass tells me today with what that photograph of me in mauve veil and hat says, I despair."

"That's from *your* point of view, whereas from mine..."

I considered Clothilde, my own mother, who said in her seventies, was I *ever* in my fifties? Clothilde, who'd give anything to see me again.

"Manon. For me, it's a tragedy," said the old Irishwoman, Keesia.

Tragedy. Somebody said to Mother Clothilde once, "She's paralyzed. That's why she's suffering all this *merde*..."

"You used a dirty word," Clothilde, our mother said.

"What?"

"Suffering." That word takes my breath away, totally silences me. She didn't use it when I was paralyzed. A pall fell between us over the telephone line like the lights being dimmed in a theatre, for curtain line.

She reminded me of Kees in this, or rather Kees reminded me of Mother. She had a commanding sense of the dramatic, the theatric gesture, voice, and timing. Holding up her one hand, Kees could gesture like Jesus stilling the waters or Moses parting the Red Sea.

When I showed her the photograph of Jacob, she said, "He looks like Jesus! Natasha's husband." And with her Irish-English accent it came out Jeeezuss, with the ringing pathos of an Anglo-Irish child during the famine.

There was nothing I could do about the effect her voice had over me.

"I have a high voice, so young," I laughed.

Her brow knit. "I sound so—old!"

"You have a resonant voice."

"I sound like a man."

Once she told me her father didn't' want to catch her crying. *But I'm a girl!* she thought—then stopped herself short. A girl of an Irish Catholic mother must be more than her sex. Her gender must transcend pain of every kind. Must have no childhood to speak of. But the Irish love the horse races. Her father took her to the races, there was some childhood then.

○

The Grand National Sweater, the crazy, wild woolly horse. At fifteen, it had caught my eye. Only when I pulled the sweater on, could I see it. *That* horse, (the palomino on the pullover cable-knit, bulky) charge*d directly* over my heart. I could hear him hoof above my ticker, my black box. Envisioned him pawing earth for carrots, for sugar. Toss his mane back in temper, snorting, "Never. Never will you canter again."

But I knew there was something in me that could not be contained. My little sister said it. "You could not be contained." They will see me in the stallion sweater (or is it a palomino that charges above my heart?) in evening, on the beach and perhaps gain heart that such feats of gymnastics can be done.

The horse would tell it differently.

I ride you—or you die.

Whether at the Grand National or the Kentucky Derby, you may be bluegrass lame but I ride you and you will not be blown, like those long wild grasses flat to the ground.

Flat to the ground, I dreamed. While time blurs many outlines, vibrant as though drawn by a sharp stiletto, the blueprint of the ward—grid, the long arm of the cross where we lay, cotted; cut across by the shorter one. It had been a summer of contagion which ended in a blur of sand on ocean and green but time crystallized, gelled in the severe, almost scriptural, terms of the ward.

Finger-to-lip, the ward spoke first one word, then two to me: the first, *Endure*, the second, *Winter*. Finger to lip, instructing myself in near silent voice. I repeated instructions to myself like a liturgy, for though I loved churches, I did not love priests or liturgy. Rather, I knew little about them being a Jewish child. But I knew I sought the love of someone utterly.

"You are a star looking for a place to shine... when you decide to come out of hiding." People said such things. But in my dream I was bucked, thrown, one, two times, 'til finally the facial bones were altered and I was no longer Velvet dreaming of the Grand National. The blue grasses that blew over me cooled me during that long sojourn of almost ten years I was lamed.

To the cold light of day I woke. No one ever knows how a pre-teen is struggling with a body, which has changed its terms.

"It doesn't bring out your beauty. Take it off!" my mother commanded.

"You are passionate and meticulous, Manon, so mind what you put on."

Bluegrass, if I could only wear it, my mother, Clothilde.

○

I noticed that if I raised both my arms the horses reared their heads. If I spread them wide, they stretched, the green nostril in one's blue head flaring. If I shrugged they shrank and twitched as if brushing off flies at some river bend.

I was inspired. Aflame.

I knew the colors were all wrong: loud red, white and blue like the flag. Never my colors.

It cost the earth—and would never be that sweater I was bundled up in and brought home from the hospital. Besides, over the past three years, from twelve to fifteen, I'd begun learning this truth: you can't go home again.

I knew I was making a crossing. A transition. From where? The hospital. But to where? The opposite bank. I went into the bedroom, closed the door where the long mirror hung. Took off the sweater, put safety pins in the shoulders to hoist them up—shoulder pads would only increase the effect of being a football player. Then the inspiration struck me to reverse it!

If I turned it round, it might not be so wild, so crazy to the eye looking at it.. Then horse would be smaller over my breast now, charging over the black box of my heart in its iron. He would be upon cream-white background. I wouldn't look so much like the flag gone berserk.

It looked worse reversed.

Revisit my options? What were my options?

Playing flute and piano duets with a friend. In the middle of our harmony, the census taker rang. "I hesitated so long to interrupt the music," she apologized. "Then why did you interrupt," I, Manon, wanted to ask, but shrugged. They cannot take a census of what goes on in the heart . My homeland is the one wild horses pawed the earth of. Here are they out to camouflage me, sabotage, to quiet my fires down?

The horse might tell it differently.

But the horse of course never got to talk. I exchanged him, knowing he was a mistake. I, Toscin-Manon, knew that. He couldn't after all blink his wool eye.

Passionate, meticulous. That's what *I* aimed to be.

○

One night, catching me considering my reflection in the mirror, she said with sorrow and quiet in her voice, our Mother, "What a bride you would have made!"

Me? In white satin and a veil?

The way she said it, with such finality in her tone, it was as though she signed its death notice. I was nineteen and had never dated a man.

I learned long ago you could veil nothing.

I blinked at the mirror. Perhaps Keesia was right. Perhaps having the use of my legs only up to age twelve, and two months, left me with vestiges of a child body, child face.

"Your face..." she said, then turned away, wind striking her cheekbone and late sun so that I saw the woman she mourned losing now that she was no longer young, was so keenly aware of age. Although for a moment—then, laughing, I shrugged off the doubts, the melancholy, the blues of a lifelong incarceration.

For a moment I felt myself relent. Would the horse sweater have emboldened me?

"Tell them," that dark husky voice, with tragic tinge, yet the light of a great actress, a Barrymore, "Tell them, you are the strength."

I turned around and he fronts me with his kind, Sepharidc Jewish eyes. "We're bringing Bright Honor home," he smiles.

Again then, I too have wanted to be desired deep down. Sought for who I am.

Where my husband was, I know not where, in those lands of mists with the drink, when he came home and socked me with his fist in my belly at the ironing board because I hadn't ironed his shirt right, I mean in those times when he was coming home in someone else's clothes, there was one American G.I. who gave me chocolates, silk hose, and cigarettes but I knew what he was really after. He considered me a mark. He was a charmer who really wanted sex with me, but I thought no, no good will come of it, he'll return overseas and it will leave me with heartache.

Kees—it was only last week—picked up the purple rose on my dining, looking up from the poster for Early Music, courtier in purple velvets strumming a lute, like our androgynous angel on the wall said, "That's what you'd look fine in, Tocsin, Renaissance velvets."

"Me?"

"Your complexion—"

I must have blushed, but that was the moment she lifted the purple rose—and I thought, will she guess it's only silk? But I fooled her! She sniffed it, then put it back.

"Only silk," I laughed. "Tell me more about the writer, the Jewish poet, who was born in London ten years before you."

When she described the gas lamps, I thought—I know those little lamps, I know the long tapers they light them with. You see, though we were born ten years apart, there were vestiges of the old left when I was an Irish Catholic child in London."

Vestiges. My legs. The wish to curl the ball of my foot over earth the way you curl your hand around a stone—becomes more intense with time.

"Tell me more about the map of London."

"It's only one square mile, London."

What I wanted to say as I looked up to meet those dark eyes—the passing of whose youth she mourned, between brown and violet a bit like velvet now near seventy—was, "You are the strength."

It was that hard, four-letter word again, work.

Then I realized—the sweater was a protective veil, a shield against the world. I no longer needed to search heaven and earth for it, just as Kees slowly began to realize she no longer had that hole in her heart, that hole she had to fill with acts of sacrifice, redemption, for she was too old for sacrifice. Her soul needed no more redeeming: it was saved.

My turn to lift the purple silk flower. Bright Honor was my name. I no longer had to hide the hole in my body. Some of the girls who'd been stricken sang *When Sonny Sings the Blues*.

"They're having a Pity Party," my mother would say.

I smiled as there shot out of the corner of my eye a child, a girl rail-thin who might have been a boy, who once was climbing trees, a girl holding her head high, skipping school, temple, the sweater on—not the one with snowflakes, which matched her spirit. Not the horse, which also matched, but was the wrong color, shape, suggestions. One plays to win. Helpers around me had worked too, but the hardest labor I'd put in myself was at age twelve and thirteen. Then I didn't shut shop on healing, I didn't check out but I put a lid on my effort and cooled my emotion.

I smiled because I knew I wasn't voiceless, powerless, but muscle of rippling bluegrass. Child is the workhorse but the horse would tell it differently. It's a tough row to hoe. They weren't bringing home a half-pint child half the weight, half the body gone. I was the strength: absolved finally, totally taken in. They were bringing Bright Honor home.

Burning: An American Dream—
A Story in Four Sections

I am the boy
That can enjoy
Invisibility.
          —Turko the Terrible

Question: How do you complete yourself?
Answer: Go with God, for you may never see this person again.

Blue Air: The Cutting Edge

Winter mornings are cut like etchings, crystal-clear. In the South, they cut clean, in the North. Mississippi delta morning or down eastern, our family lived at the edge, pushing the envelope. Dislocation, location was the name of our game. How can one overinvest in a child who burns herself on purpose to excise the deeper, psychic pain?

"It's the sort of weather that sets my spirit on edge," says Erin with her Norman face, round, then again in some lights, sculptural like Rembrandt in one of his late self-portraits, Hamlet of Holland.

When Sabine heard her sister was having a hard time, she pulled out of her top drawer, two of her grandmother's heirlooms, turning them in the light. Her sister's daughter was *drop dead beautiful*! Tamara, at the cutting edge, working out. She seemed to carry that brilliance. However she turned, she took the breath away. A Jewish beauty, with an almost Egyptian profile. Her complexion was luminous blue-white, like porcelain. Offsetting charcoal hair was her creamy, ivory skin. Her claim to fame was ballet from the age of nine. She had danced, at age thirteen, a special ballet choreographed for her of Anne Frank. "The hopeful side to Anne," she'd said to Aunt Sabine. The grace of her hand sprang from that in her heart. It was when the pressure began to build until at age thirteen, she crashed and burned. She tore her mask off, bleached her hair blond, wore platform shoes, Barbie doll clothing, tons of pancake makeup and eye shadow, had her belly-button pierced and a ring put in, had her eyebrows cut and a rhinestone set in.

A month later the sky broke open. She slit her belly causing her own blood to run. To her horror, her parents discovered it when Tam raised her arms. There were twenty-two small razor slits.

The color red shone now on the white stainless air of the clinic for child eating disorders: scarlet shone in the numerous waiting rooms, hung with artwork, of child psychiatrists. Tam was still razor-thin and had begun to smoke up a storm.

"Are you able to cry?" Sabine asked her sister.

"I can't," said Magda. Then added quietly, "If I have to die, I'll go into a corner and do it."

It was the American disease, her mother Magda learned. Seemingly without pain, Tamara did it again and again, beginning the morning in blazing blue July when she turned fourteen. She was a classic case. There were ten episodes in one year. Hardly had her abdomen heal before it was incised again.

Zoloft was the new kid on the block, one of the anti-depressants a friend recommended to Magda when Tam was close to fifteen. Last year, in Spain where Magda had taken Tam in exile, they'd gone through milk laced with whiskey. Back in the States, Tamara smoked a pack a day. The air was blue. "Nails to a coffin" her older sister called it. Like a blue dragon, hunched, thin, it was dwelling in Tamara's bedroom. Other nights, she'd drink a sleeve of beer to draw off the tension with the kids downtown Austin.

At her new prep school in New England, which specialized in the arts, winding paths were gardened. By the third week, a senior had looped his arm around her waist. Her mother, Magda listened to the October birds, finch and woodpecker, hammering away at the bark outside her bedroom. Angular herself, thin—Tam was her reflection—Magda knew guilt of the survivor.

Frosty, the temperature had dropped to below freezing. Cold bit like a dog, or a saw. The last wounds of childhood shone in the hatchet marks on trees.

Sabine, Tamara's aunt, had been disabled from the age twelve where polio left her in a wheelchair. Now, she wore her Irish jacket, which came up to her chin. Coming home had epitomized all homecoming, its memories etched on the calendar every last Thursday of November, harvesting the bounty survival.

Boys Who Die Virgin

Rare was the boy of seventeen who was virgin. There were teenage boys, barely fourteen, who weren't virgin. Most of the fourteen-year-olds were not broken in. But they were not spotless as the unborn lamb. When they'd taken a girl, the last ones to know it were their mothers. Sam was one of those who made the break through at nearly fourteen, but his mother didn't know. Sam with dark eyes and glasses who looked the picture of the little professor. But then Sam was to die young. Before his fourteenth birthday dawned.

Allie relived childhood deaths as she turned her grandmother's jewels in the winter sunlight, wondering what profit they could turn. Allie, her doctor, had lost her older boy on a camping trip. Allie's two boys, Thom and Sam, were eleven and almost fourteen. The trip to the caves had been a pre-fourteenth birthday gift. She'd bought his fourteenth birthday bike—a ten-speed mountain bike—and hid it in the potting shed.

The night before had been Friday the thirteenth, mid-October featuring a red full harvest moon burning up, like so much paper, Sam had brown eyes, giving away his adoption. "There's no way I could be your kid... I don't resemble any one in our family."

He'd just taken up tuba in junior high band. When *Amazing Grace* came over the radio, he said "That's what I want played at my funeral, Mom." For years Allie couldn't listen to the hymn without tears: the cold brass bell of the tuba at Christmas.

On the camping trip, they asked permission, the brothers. They found some caves. Some loose dirt avalanched tons. Sam had already started to crawl in. His brother saw him disappear before his eyes, saw his orange hat roll down the hill. Then the earth avalanched like a huge beige animal shedding his skin. When they dragged Sam out, his pulse was twenty per minute. His mother rowed with him and holding his head in her lap. When they got to the hospital, they jump-started his heart twice. If he lived he would be brain-damaged. Allie looked at her husband, standing in the hospital rook. He looked like Abe Lincoln six foot five tall, his lank frame folding.

Her husband shook his head.

First they thought to fly home to Oklahoma, Pawnee, Allie's birth land, but when they began driving to New Mexico, they also began slowly healing. In Albuquerque they changed clothes, then drove into Pawnee to bury him. Just as they were crossing the city line, the car radio said, "New Mexico boy killed in landslide over the week-end."

They said she was magnificent at the funeral, Allie. Sabine relives it now in frames of a waking vision. The doctor had been forty-one.

Thomas, the boy who survived, had nightmares for a long time. In these dreams, he was all out there, on his own like on a cliff at the edge of the world, the universe. He began burning himself, which his parents only found out about later. There was the link with Tam. Tam's self inflicted tiny cigarette burns on her belly and arms had reopened the vein of Sam's death, his brother's self inflicted wounds. In the middle of the night, he came to his parents although he was a tall boy over eleven. But nobody could sleep with Thom; he turned circles in his sleep. They put his sleeping bag on the floor beside their bed in the cabin up the desert canyon, the home built with their own hands of cedar and pine, tongue-in-groove logs. The boys shared a bedroom until they turned eight and ten. Thomas kept a teddy bear on his pillow when they had bunk beds. Sam kept a frog with splay-legs, Kermit, on his upper bunk.

The day Sam reached the two-digit age he said, "Now I'll never go back." With horn-rimmed glasses perched upon thin bridge of his nose, over dark-brown eyes, he spoke with a low alto voice as toddler, like a foghorn. Strangers mistook it for gloom.

Thom reverted to being very young. He sat in his mother's lap, big, twelve. He failed sixth grade. The weight of this death carved into him. Carving moot consolation out of Thom's behavior, Sabine relived this time more deeply. With Thom, like with Tamara, it was his mother who first discovered the blood. Allie and Magda, two Magdalene's.

"Looks like blood on your seat, sugar," she said one morning when he got up from the wood chair in the kitchen. Sam shrugged, left to start fooling around in the tool-shed behind the kitchen. Then she discovered blood on his socks.

The places he chose for were the tender skin between his toes, and his duff. Thom had another secret. He alone, knew that Sam hadn't died a virgin.

But he wasn't the one who'd slipped Sam the rubber behind the barn.
Sarah, Sarah,
Down South,
What's your real name? Tell us with your honeyed mouth.

Magda Rubin slipped out of slacks into winter nightgown, flicked off the light. Tam was still down the hall studying, she could see her shadow projected on the wall, a profile.

There was another kind of cutting; the good kind. The etching Jack Frost created on starry winter nights so that when you woke at the crack of dawn you cried, in the blinding sparkling air, *Jubilate!*

Magda looked at her daughter bent over homework in winter light. She'd spoken last night of returning to the dance, "I didn't burn myself when I was doing gymnastics, mom."

Her daddy was flying out with all her ballet gear: portable barre, leotards, and toe slippers plus boom box. Tonight, in the lamplight, her delicate Jewish star earrings counterpointed the silver flash of snow whenever head lamps of a passing car shone upon it, then the road was plunged back into blackness. Magda went into reverie. But the child's scoliosis discovered just last summer threw her into a state of fear. She thought of her sister, Sabine's, disability. She took Tam to a yoga master an acupuncturist, a chiropractor and a massage therapist.

Where lay sanctuary? Was all this the blood that must come with birth? A rite of passage? Would they find a less dark baptism here in the Massachusetts woods where Tam was exactly one year older than Juliet when she fell in love with Romeo?

Initiation: Rite, Sanctuary

"Would you rather have been a boy?" Nicole asked Tam one morning when Tam is practicing pirouettes.

"Who, me?" she piped back. "I'm too busy."

"Too busy?"

"Sorry, Mom. I wasn't paying attention. A boy! Then I'd have to lift women in ballet."

Until she entered puberty, which meant wearing a sports bra, Tam had the long torso of a boy, the slender hips, and the incredible ability to fold and unfold into chairs, boy-long.

One December night, after the clinic for childhood-depression, Magda found the letter from Tam's boyfriend. Tam had left her diary face-side-up on her desk when she dashed to get the phone, Against her will, Magda let her eyes rove across the sheet of meticulously formed words her daughter had received.

Dearest Tam,

Considering we've only known each other so short a time—I am surprised to be overwhelmed by my feelings. I dream of your profile day and night.

What happened in the car last weekend, if you are pregnant, I'll pay for the abortion.

        Yours in truest trust,
        Ben

Magda phoned her gynecologist and set up an appointment for tomorrow afternoon. She phoned her husband. Her older daughter, Nicole was the one they counted on to take Tam for the examination. Zoloft, Magda had only been taking the drug two weeks. It hadn't kicked in. She always grew impatient for it to kick in and abandoned the drug to try another one.

Sabine, unknowing of this, thought about her Irish friend Erin and the nuns.

In the northern woods, where the woodpecker had been, Magda watched snowfall and glimpsed her fifteen-year-old, a sapling Dante in the kitchen dipping her nose in a sleeve of beer. She'd decided to defer mentioning Ben's letter for tomorrow morning. Instinctively, the air slightly blue in the kitchen, Magda closed her eyes and saw crimson.

What strange muse had touched her daughter's shoulder at birth making her fragile as silk, yet silk-strong? Tamara became a warrior, an emotional flame-thrower at age eleven? A potentially great ballerina at age thirteen. She'd begun to do extensions effortlessly at the six o'clock positions when twelve. Yet her soul was being dislocated all the while.

When Nicole phoned from the gynecologists' office at four p.m., she had laughter in her voice.

"Mom," she reported, "Take a deep breath. Tam's a virgin!"

Magda felt her jaw drop. A reddish sun was setting. She felt thorned in. Numb. This was followed immediately by a sensation of pins and needles in arms and legs. She'd lied to Tam, never getting to the revelatory letter. Tamara said, "You don't mean the burns, mom, because for that I've got Dr. Wallenstein."

Dr. Annie Wallenstein in Somerville was now the custodian of her Tamara's mental health, a specialist. A doctor at Wellesley had recommended her. Annie Wallenstein required self-abusers to enter a contract with her, signing and dating how long they'd gone between episodes. Accountability was her key.

In her kitchen up north, mirroring her sister's kitchen down south in the woods, Sabine looked once more at the pearl earrings turning them to catch the tints under the lamp.

To relieve her mind of fear over Tamara, Sabine relived the time with Allie and Sam. Sam was no virgin.

It wasn't a girl his age, there was no question of rape or robbing the cradle.

It was an older girl at the Baptist Sunday School, Renee, who at fifteen had asked eleven-year-old Sam to come into her room to help with math homework. He was skinny, tall for his age. She was overdeveloped at fifteen. She'd put his thin lanky hand on her partridge-plump bosom. Quick as a wink, she was slipping out of skirt and sweater—yanked over her head. "I can please you, Sam," she said, "Like you've never been pleased before." She slipped him a rubber, the thing his brother should have done. It was a scene typically southern.

He was scared and excited.

It came and went fast. Like a streak of lightning. His heart pounded like it would burst his rib cage. Nobody could have foreseen that the next week he would be cannonball into eternity, without breathing a word about losing his virginity.

He'd planned how he'd tell his baby brother. He'd spin it out as a yarn acting nonchalant all the time. He'd scored. Renee told him he'd brought her over the top.

His mother asked, "Cat got your tongue?"

Allie being a doctor-mom, was there any inkling she might have smelled it on him?

Closure: The Boy

Erin with her dark, comforting voice spoke words of solace to her grandson. Wherever you go, go with God, her throaty voice seemed to say... the angel in the inkwell was her sole companion.

Allie's family? Thom, Nick and childhood photographs of Sam now he was gone. Seth his favorite cousin had been one of the pallbearers in Oklahoma last month. To be forever locked ten yards out side Ferris' Oyster Bar and Lady Mae Costumes, a child by a beautiful ocean is the paralyzed person's term of existence.

Sabine's family...Pascal with whom she enjoyed a sleeve of Warsteiner in the evenings. She lived in the company of women. Erin down the block, the Irishwoman who said, "When I was president of the Cancer Society I learned how many people drink in evening."

Nicole was a knockout, not drop dead beautiful like her kid sister Tamara, but she turned heads: with her height, she was five-foot-seven, her golden skin and chestnut hair with long glossy gold-red strands from the sun.

Magda reflected on her daughters, the tall one and the gifted air. She meditated upon burning one's own skin, a bizarre disorder which, nonetheless, the American disease, oddly reflected the inverted American Dream. With her two Jewish daughters, the exotic Tamara, the radiantly American as apple-pie Nicole, she felt the dislocation, which washed over her as a child, then again as a young woman on this blue planet. Head bowed, she was back in girlhood where she saw the cored apple, like white wood, on the table, the small dish of brown sugar.

She caught Tam from the corner of her eye. "Get a grip on yourself, Tamara. You're lighting up and you've already got one dangling by your lip."

This provoked a smile, then a slow laugh from Tamara. She rose, stubbed out both Silva Thins in the glass dish, stretched, and yawned like a cat, her tee shirt pulling up over her long waist revealing her navel. Tamara who had beauty to die for, ran her long fingers through her bobbed dark hair, and began to hum under her breath.

"What's that you're humming?" her mother shot her eyebrows up.

Alabama, can it be your light and power are failing?

"Just a tune," Tam shrugged. Tamara was becoming invisible to herself, Tam was walking fence rails. The first little cigarette burn she gave herself was the worst. She drew her breath in high wire tension. Those incredibly long lashes slightly singed by nicotine. Like in a dream, Tamara extended both hands in an incredibly elegant *port de bras*, the movement that had silenced the assembly in the Holocaust Museum last year in when she'd portrayed Anne Frank. Eyes half-closed, hands held forth, she glided out of the kitchen, flicking off the wall-light, following her inborn theatrical impulse, casting her gaze back across her shoulder. Burning. It continued until, like the Civil War, the self-destruction set the whole map of American on flame.

She wasn't thinking of her mother and sister. They had disappeared. She saw the night outside, smoke-silver. She'd learned an elation. It wasn't a girl-thing like dress up or a boy-thing like hunting. This was ecstasy. There is, thought Magda, no way I can have different expectations of Tamara or reach this child totally. She is not of this earth. There's no way I'd want to pull her back from being at the edge, pushing the envelope. Tamara is chameleon, liquid in movement, like water never to be held in one place.

Into Sabine's daydream comes the Irishwoman's voice, a bit guttural, the rasp of a ghetto child, one raised during the Blitz in London, saying, "Go with God You may never pass this way again." Tamara was way out there, with the American dream of the white steeple cleaving the stark blue sky mackerel clouds rolling in, each strip of sky like wood in a boat, the blinding steeple every now and then harpooning a cloud. Dislocation, it cut all their lives, no matter where their location.

What Tamara hummed was the tune, which was her own child, her brainchild, her dream-child, she moved wrist out with body the long fingers tapered like birds in flight, the grace borne out into her hand from her heart. Tamara, with her ashen complexion, and her soprano girl's voice before it deepens and matures, it was a melody which she'd made up—with her quicksilver ways.

I am the boy
That can enjoy
Invisibility

Alabama, Long Gone

Maturity, which is fatal to so many enchantments, had not been able to dislodge her from her pedestal.
                Mark Twain, *The Facts Concerning the Recent Carnival of Crime in Connecticut*

Setting Out the Costume

Ours is the generation that lays out its clothes the night before. Brown hose, gold turtleneck, and the brown skirt. Either for school then, or for work now, or for just plain living, another day rolling comfortingly around. Or, if the day contains threat, some menacing unknown, at least it's a comfort to know your clothes are laid out besides the radiator knocking, the clock ticking.

Whose generation? Yours and mine, the war generation although you grew up on one side, I on the other of the Atlantic ocean. While Erika writes, my stories flow as smoothly as her river, the smoothness is in her life, not in mine. The truth is I'm having trouble booking our flight to Texas. All the schedules are printed up but I'm confused. It's unlike me to be confused by such a thing, unlike me to shilly-shally, which tells me my heart's in some sort of trouble over this projected voyage at American Thanksgiving.

I've started to lie over it—which is a bad sign. I don't mind the hotel in the airport whereas it struck terror into both our hearts, tapping the hidden fear all humans have of being trapped. There's no way to get out, a thing which unnerved me too: rooms overlook a swimming pool, glassed in. There would literally be no safe and speedy exit from a disaster like fire, or earthquake.

Could there be such a thing as a carnival of crime? Were evil thoughts possible?

I would more happily rise to put on war's clothing. At least I've had the guts to write my brother-in-law. I'm lukewarm, at best, overcoming, dearly as I love our mother, how can I explain I'm willing to have God come for her without seeing her one more time? But time is on my side, not hers. I *should* want to fly down. I'm even willing to hear my sister cry out that she'll never forgive me, never love me again if I renege on what's probably our last chance at a family reunion. I know she'll forgive me, and we've never had a good family reunion.

"It's hard not to believe it's on purpose," Magda, my sister, says of some marital exclamations.

I have set out the picture of my beloved at age five in France to calm me down. She squats before an old tree, beside her brother, both on solid legs, both slightly frowning. There's that characteristic determination in the set of her moth, and it's typical of her that her stout feet are planted wide in white shoes, a swatch of her strikingly dark navy-blue underpants showing.

Glancing about for a passage from a cherished book, I pull out My Vegetable Love: A Journal of a Growing Season, an enchanting and out-of-the way journal, for our twenty-seventh anniversary. Out of it slips a bookmark with Magda's phone numbers scrolled on it: Magda in France, Madga at home, Magda's cell phone—for on the road and all times. Magda in her new experiment in living, Massachusetts, the very core of New England was like a story book of its own, with coffee shop, gas station, post office. Opening my address book, I have in addition to these four or five recent phone numbers for my sister. Magda in Manhattan—this one written in ink, for the summer she and Tam rented a shoebox apartment in New York so that Tam could study at the American Ballet Theatre, one of the youngest dancers ever to enroll in their courses.

The clothing laid out the night before: so comforting.

"I've got brown hose to go with the fabulous skirt," the slightly raspy voice of Erin comes over the phone. "They're all laid for tonight so that if I come home more tired than I know not what, I can just slip into 'em. I'm appalled by how big I've become."

"When people give up smoking, that's what sometimes happens," I try.

"Like—Scarlet O'Hara, I'll have to say, 'What the future brings it will bring.'"

"I think you look terrific."

"That's not the point: zippers won't do up, buttons, nor anything. Maybe it's a matter of exercise."

It troubled me that her cigarette cough was back again—like everyone's in Ireland.

When Francis met me for lunch today, I could tell by her face, it was grim news. Her sister's cancer recurring? She bore sombre, autumnal flowers: winter mums. Quietly, she told me it's gone to the neck and spine.

How different from Pat, our woman gardener, who came to transplant our two small trees. She came in smiling, a wide grin, in fact, one sprung from ear-to-ear, despite having lost it with her nineteen-year-old son over the weekend.

"Another funeral," she said.

"I'm sorry," I began, realizing my mistake. In my profession, sorry?— "It put food on the table for two weeks."

The happy funerals take place in my mind, while Erika's morning e-mail comes into my hand. Her storyteller friend, Emma, is there for the weekend. Her daughter, like Magda's, suffered deep depression after giving up gymnastics, which was her world.

When I gave up my legs, it was not the world I gave up, but exchanged one for another, like slipping off an article of clothing—fine as an article of faith—a very filmy one for another which let perhaps more of the world in, but less of the soul out. So in a narrow space I taught myself, I slowly, painstakingly learned, a new language of moving. This is my white water: a thing Erin must know, but not necessarily my sister Magda, nor my lover.

The only other soul on earth who treads water this painstakingly could well be Erin. Is there any way I can tell these young women this thing? The resilience is the parent, not the daughter. So perhaps Magda is right in saying what I don't want to admit: 'her tragedy, my child.'"

Emma's family doctor sent them with their troubled daughter, Val, to the Hinks Institute of Child Psychology in Toronto, which helped her out of the pit. Shall I suggest it to my sister? I must tread carefully these days when I would understand my brother-in-law being hurt by my telling him coming to Texas rings a dim chord in me, if any.

Yet that leaden image is true to my heart's core.

Fanfare

"I would be demented if I had to go three weeks without a computer," said Erin this morning. She who's shot me a sidelong glance at lunch the other day telling me what I already knew, "I can be mean."

"Well, I ask myself, can I still think—the answer is I can."

Nonetheless, a forceful alto down the hall is bellowing, "Yours is hooped," still unnerves me from this morning. In the beginning the way she threw around computer language made me think of putting on the dog: "Booting up," a "technophobe," and so on. Now I simply accept it as the language she can toss off being comfortable, familiar with it. Me? Put me eye to eye with a person, set me on any human terrain and I have faith I won't stumble.

"Those without faith," my friend, Frances, whose sister's cancer has returned, said at lunch, "have more, what shall I call it?—Compassion."

Now, the computer begins to sound what I can only call a fanfare of brass, reminding me of *Fanfare for the Common Man*, Copeland's. It's brassy, like a flourish of trumpets, sounds every few lines. Erika, your river may be flowing smoothly today—but not this life of mine. And only yesterday, Erin told me, "Yours is the most maligned religion."

Brown skirt, golden turtleneck, brown hose to top it all off. Only she ran a ladder from stem-to-stern, Erin, the other morning so could I not wear the brown skirt.

"But you know what?" she said. "It'll be there for this evening."

She tells me that when Min, her Chinese cleaning woman was picked up by her husband last night on the dot of six p.m., she saw his new van. "It's ironic, I hate to use the term workin' class but…"

"Blue collar worker," I interjected, hopefully, wanting to hear no classicist comments, although she was from England.

"Yes, that's the word I was lookin' for. We're more—educated. If it's blue, it's blue hose!"

Chuckling.

She comes in with news of the resident manager, Matty Smart, an Englishwoman, her close friend.

"Mrs. Brodie was taken in an ambulance to the Emergency Room yesterday mawning. A pipe burst in Mr. Migilacutty's suite. Who knows, yours could be next…and so on…and so on…Matty phoned me up…"

So, sighing, once again I hear the gory details, the bloody ones this time. We are back, feeling rich in a London childhood, as above a Cockney one.

Which drew me back to where I'm best, a girlhood, upstate New York morning. There was my white puff-sleeved blouse with the pearl buttons down the front, the blouse freshly pressed. There was my plaid skirt with suspenders because I was so thin, and there were the dark woolen knee socks, scratch, but my legs stout enough to hold them up. The radiator was banging, the radio was on with war news in the kitchen, static coming through more than information. It was 1944.

Erin, too, was waking to a similar morning, in London. The Blitz had left her world leveled. "I thought we were poor," she told me this morning over the phone, "but when I saw the Cockneys, those without any refrigeration and with only torn badly patched clothin'—I knew how rich we were."

The other afternoon, over-tired—largely, I imagined from the weight of dragging her left arm around—useless, paralyzed and heavier with the years no doubt, she'd sat at my kitchen table and announced as plainly as she'd announced the rain would continue, "I'm losin' weight. I hope Kathleen doesn't put me through the mill this afternoon over the apartment I found her, 'cause I can feel I'm not long on patience."

"Indeed," I had come to echo her.

"But in a way, I think I'm dealin' with a demented person."

"Why?"

"She feels so hounded, she phoned late last night to ask would her heavy dining set, it's oak, of table and four chairs go through the floor."

"Are you serious, Kathleen?" I asked.

Said Erin, "I am."

"Kathleen," I explained, "There's a retainin' wall and four solid inches of plaster in your place."

So Kathleen had been calmed down.

The very first call I receive after removing my trees from our planter, as Council requested me to, is a phone call from our downstairs neighbor, "Isn't the fall weather fine? I'm phoning about your trees outside your living room window. They're leaking on me."

I thought back to the feisty girl I was who lived outside the Alabama Light & Power Company.

I rung off knowing I'd resolved one key thing: I wouldn't even try to go to Texas. I'd e-mail my brother-in-law, to soften the blow, to save my shame? No, I was operating at a handicap. Time to call the shots: no longer able to wake each morning, go to sleep each night, between a rock and a hard place. In saying this, I wouldn't be giving up on the love between my mother and me. Nor would I be saying, "This family has lost visits from this member to a childhood disease." Far more complex, many-layered in its pain and implications was my decision.

It was then that I myself began to feel I had taken vows. The blue hose and blue clothes shot through my mind. After she left, I'd lie down. There's a phrase "Spine-to-feathers." I used to round it out this way: "Spine-to-feathers and dream of you." Now I began to feel I would lose it. So as I type this afternoon on the keyboard that isn't "hooped", and the fanfare continues to blare in my ear, I recall now...

It's true, just this past weekend, my brother-in-law, Joshua Rubin, Joshua, Jewish, like all our family, returned from Munich. He dared breathe there! He told me he stood on the very terrace Hitler had ranted and raved from. It felt triumphant and odd that three Jewish musicians should stand in that very room, on that very terrace from which the unintelligible rantings of a fanatic, a maniac were broadcast round the earth to the free world. Josh, you have been there where the Munich Manikins were. You who humor our eighty-five year old mother by buying her "100's" when she asked you for cigarettes at the end of what has been an exasperating evening.

It wasn't in Radio-Free Europe, it wasn't in England, either, that I heard them. It was at home in our tiny little upstate New York town bordering Canada, Plattsburgh on Lake Champlain. Tense, a child of five, for whom no world was foolproof, I hunkered up to the radio with my Papa Louis, and caught what words I could. My swallowing was hard. When Poppa turned to me one ominous and awesome evening, and said in his lyrical Russian accent, "It's over, dolling."

"What, Papa?" I asked, swallowing hard in my worship, my adoration of him.

"The war. The war in Europe."

"Does that mean burning up Jews is over? No more children tossed up in the air and shot, Papa? No more kids like me shoveled in big iron shovels into the live flames?"

But he could not answer. He took me in his arms. We both began sobbing. He first, for my adoration of him manifested itself in my reflecting whatever he was doing, as though I, the small, thin, tense child were a mirror of my Russian grandfather's great years on earth.

It extended the set of clothes from either Erin's or mine. I was twelve years old. My legs had been taken away for life. It was a still winter morning. "When do I get to wear the pink gingham?"

"That's for Sunday when your folks come—if they come," the nurse sniffed to me.

"They will," I assured her. It was then, as she turned on her heels, I overheard what I never should have: "That one's bold, such confidence! She's sassy, I'd say. But let me tell you, I won't be *Jewed* out or down."

I'd never heard the phrase before the night nurse barked it angrily, behind my back (or so she thought) that one time. I knew, however, instantly what it meant the first, as I did, the second time.

I loved Erin for her maturity, that winning attraction. I loved it—how she bore up under the funeral of her grandson's playmate—even though he was pallbearer last summer for his friend. I even loved it that Erin smoked again—in a way, making her more the *femme fatale*, the sophisticated European; magnetic, being endowed with temperament, nerved—as opposed to nervous. I loved it that she returned my every call, and in that mellifluous voice said, "No need to return this one, Sharon," relieving me of unnecessary formalities and tasks, making me more able to focus on the task at hand.

But that she used this word?

The *Swastika* flashed upon my eye: I covered my eyes, emotionally, as at a flash of gunfire.

I grew chill down to my fingertips—my legs were cold all the time anyway. It was a December evening. I began shivering in my bed. There was no one I could tell. Not my cubicle-mate when she returned from late treatment, nor the kid fresh out of the operating room. (This was a reflection of the unsafe world I'd known at age five and six during the war, not a mirror-image, but a more sombre, dusky reflection.) Not another night nurse, she'd think I was a sissy, ratting. And never, ever as long as I lived my parents.

That's why, when I heard it yesterday morning from her very lips, Erin's, my blood turned cold again. Alabama, your light and power are failing.

Erin, I can see you wearing your Mogen David as clearly as I can under the crucifix hung over your mother's bedroom doorway. You go, your hand in the river's these nights. You go also with the tiny fellow of nicotine lit-up, cheerily glowing. If you don't take care, you will go no longer your hand in mine.

Of course, she meant it as an indictment of those who used it. "If I ever hear you use that phrase again—" and she said the hateful phrase.

Trembling

Her using it brought back upon me that fit of childhood trembling. I'd hit my arm with the other arm to stop the trembling. Like the phrase, I'd forgot entirely about, this spasm.

It went so far that I worshipped his spastic hands, Papa Louis. He had Parkinson's. He'd roll a Black Russian himself, then light the match. He'd tilt his vodka in a saucer without spilling a drop, but passing it—as tenderly as he might a kiss—to his lips. Enchanted, I'd watch the flame trembling, trembling.

That's how it connects to the final, crucial clothes laid out for me that winter of polio.

Not my gingham dress, the safe, the known. The girls have not gathered for a pity party for themselves but for the dolls.

Not the tank suits of scratch wool they'd boil us in, in stainless steel burning Hubbard Tanks, in the hospital basement.

Not the winding sheet, the color of mil, that twelfth summer of my life might have become. Like the look on Francis' face today at lunch—when she brought the sombre winter mums and I knew it announced death, that look: that her sister's cancer had returned. Ironically, the face of the woman gardener returned saying, "Don't grieve, not in our profession: a funeral is food on my table for two weeks."

Not any of these sombre colors, nor these whites, the garment that returns. Loitering with love, I remember it. After all, I went to school down South where the hygiene teacher said to nine-year-olds, you're still knee-high to a grasshopper, but girls, when you start applying cosmetics, remember to wash your puffs." We had two nipples and a fuff. Fanny was a girl's name but not mentioned as the part of your body you sat on.

It reminded me of something muslin—virginal, annunciatory: it might have been a girl's first communion lace because it was white. Only it wasn't a communion white, nor a bridal gown. It was changed every morning, then again as sun set winter-red, and iron colors claimed the rest of that span of consciousness, turning it into night.

It was our plain, starched hospital gown: the one each of us children was given, with New York State Rehabilitation Center stamped on it, reminiscent of those blue numbers injected under the skin at Auschwitz.

What does the chalice of bedlam hold tonight? Little star grains white as barley beads, or beads of mercury or dark salt crystals?

Even at this juncture of half a century, I think there's no one I can tell my feeling not of hatred but affection for these gowns which wrapped us every morning, every evening. Not even Erin, whose maturity is her fatal attraction, who survived the Blitz—whose clothing she lays out for herself every evening for the day to come. "Jewed out." What a hideous phrase. No, nor Magda, my sister, who turns from all memory of that perilous time when I was stricken. It is as though she spiritually covers her ears.

But, wait, perhaps there is one—perhaps only Erika, for whom the smoothly flowing river is not a symbol for life. Why her? I could possibly tell her, because she knows life is far more often white water than smooth water. She would surely understand there was comfort in a child knowing her white gown would be laid out for morning; the days were not random. They were severe, highly regimented. But you knew what pain, what grief would come down.

Shivering at the word I heard that half a century ago, and just yesterday morning, I decide, yes, Erika would be my confidante: my one and only person for this telling. My purpose for being born—one of my purposes—this telling. After all, it was she who translated with me the "last Jewish poet to write in German."

In the light bulb-blue light of dawn—not collar and stockings of that hue—but the stiff gown, still hot from the huge steam irons of the institution, this would be the laying out of clothes to wholly cover, like the vows a novice takes—as pain and shame are covered, and death at the very end—the novitiate of ten or twelve, at the outside of thirteen.

Down south the screens were a mess of sorrowful grey grid with rips that let flies in. Up north, we lathered and lathered our screens like a woman at scrub board, the old metal and wood ones, lathering and lathering to beat out of the body the sorrows of her marriage, her son. There were wood irons. The last battle of the woh' of no'thern aggression. The Baptist preacher shouted about something called the kingdom of heaven, which was like a mustard seed, which became greater than all herbs, and shot forth branches. But I saw more the sick looking at foods and not tasting pleasure because of her pain. And I could tell Mother saw. She nodded.

What a man would give his right nut for up north and down south were two different things. Basically it boiled down to up north was more education, more things like book reviews. Down south, a quick grab, a Kewpie doll. But then again, mystification set in because Eulalie-Sue after all used the saying "right nut" for an appearance in the Atlanta Times which her daddy, the journalist, would have given back in 1947.

Alabama Light & Power Co

Alabama, I must finally admit that you are broken but never submit the cruelty of you, Alabama the state. It was as if there was a camera everywhere filming at the outer limits of life.

Beside the loading platform, down south in the Alabama hot night winds, stood the Alabama Light & Power Company. So it was long ago in Alabama. The heart divided in two. And if it was that way in Alabama, it must have been that ways in other corners of the globe.

On the bed in granny Fay's bedroom stood a one hundred year old doll, hands clenched before her as if she harnessed all the light and power in those tiny clenched fists, necessary for the kingdom. I'd been writing and writing and writing. My pocket book, my parachute was still mysterious to me but I knew its ways far more than I did at the beginning of my ninth year. My bisque doll that had held the chalice of Bedlam never came back whole: her face looked always as if half of it had been sliced off.

Before their findings were ready for publication, seventeenth-century astronomers transposed them into Latin anagrams: rearranged letters of a word or phrase to produce a new word or phrase, using all of the original letters exactly once. Anagrams exist throughout our language as links between words and phrases. *Silent* becomes *Listen*; *Astronomer* becomes *Moon Starer*; *Narcissism* becomes *Man's Crisis*. "*La Cucina mia,*" I said not knowing the Latin. In the darkness, the proverbial babe in the woods, we were finding new markings.

Why were you smashed, Alabama, when you held all that light and power? Was it passed on to me? In the South, the visible and invisible came together for a brief moment, flickered light shining upon Harmony Gas Works, The Printorium, the Euphoria Bricker Layers Union#29. Then it plunged the earth into a deeper blackness than it had ever know. Once in a blue moon, invisible and visible came together, balanced for a precarious moment and made sense of the world. Married. We were given no shadow to nest under.

Alabama was long gone: her face shattered in shards, her expression broken. I looked down at the gap in the slat boards. Here we were, Christless in Silentville again. Yet there was a stirring. The last sun became a different animal. The story is now. And it's big. The features of the doll blur together as under water or through flame. Her face is a maze of tiny veins. Eulalie-Sue's mother's words come back to me, "Jesus, all I want is a safe crossing."

The passage, this hero's rite of passage, and this very difficult long journey. This could be the crack in the world through which the light shines.

ANTHOLOGIES
The Sorrow Psalms: A Book of Twentieth Century Elegy
(University of Iowa Press)
Crazed by the Sun: Poems of Ecstasy (Cyber wit Academic Press)
[Forthcoming]   *Magical Kites: Childhood's Inner Voices*
Forgiveness: The Final Furlough

Books by Lynn Strongin

POETRY
The Dwarf Cycle (Thorp Springs Press)
Shrift (Thorp Springs Press)
Countrywoman/Surgeon (L'Epervier Press)
Nightmare of Mouse (L'Epervier Press)
Toccata of the Disturbed Child (Fallen Angel Press)
Paschal Poem (Sunring Press)
A Hacksaw Brightness (Ironwood Press)
The Birds of the Past Are Singing (Cross-Cultural Communications)
The Girl with Copper Colored Hair (Conflux Press)
Wyves of the Fire Dye (Last Heron Press)
Rembrandt's Smock (Plain View Press)
The Cobalt Horse (Conflux Press)
Dvorak's Rose (Last Heron Press)
The Medici Girls (Last Heron Press)
Twin Tan Dogs: A Mystical Bestiary
The Dreamlife of Foxes & Swans (Last Heron Press)
Rambunction (Last Heron Press)
Cape Seventy (Thorp Springs Press)
Dark Salt (Casa de Snapdragon) -first in upcoming trilogy
[Forthcoming}   *Secrets You Tell Your Doll*
               Orphan Stars
               The Lesson Longest Learned

POETRY BOOKS with photos by Penelope Weiss
Barn Falling Down: A Winter Lens (Last Heron Press)
Portraits in Glass and Light (Last Heron Press)

FICTION & MEMOIR
Bones & Kim, a novella (Spinster's Ink Press)
That Glorious Child, Fynn (Casa de Snapdragon)
Albino Peacock: Tales of a Southern Jewish Girlhood (Plain View Press)
Star Quilt: The Seventh Jump (Plain View Press)
Nikko's Child (Conflux Press)
Indigo: A Poet's Childhood (Thorp Springs Press)
Spectral Freedom (Casa de Snapdragon)
Obliquities (Cyberwit Academic Publisher, India)
Dovey & Me (Solo Press)

About the Cover Artist

Cover artist Mark Heine comes from a family of renowned Canadian artists. In his 30-year career in the arts, Heine's work has been shown throughout North America and Europe. His art is now held in private collections worldwide, including that of author Lynn Strongin, one of his largest collectors. Heine lives in Victoria, B.C., Canada with his partner Lisa and their children Sarah and Charlotte.

See his work at www.markheine.com.

About the Author

Born in New York City in 1939, Lynn Strongin was raised in and around New York. California was home during the politically active sixties and Albuquerque, New Mexico, in the seventies. She has lived in British Columbia since 1979, although she considers herself profoundly to be an American writer.

Lynn Strongin is one of the most frequently heard voices in the American classroom. Nominated for the Pulitzer Prize, in 2010, she is a five-time-Pushcart Prize nominee, and has been nominated twice for the prestigious

Griffin Award for Excellence in Poetry. Her most recent books are *That Glorious Child, Fynn* (Casa de Snapdragon Press), *Dark Salt, A Brush with Genius* (J.B. Sillwater Publishing Co) and *Albino Peacock* "tales of a Jewish Southern girl (Plain View Press.) *Alabama Light & Power Co* is a product of a southern girlhood and has been in the hopper thirty years. It is her fifth book published with Plain View Press. Among forthcoming projects is her trilogy forthcoming from J.B. Stillwater Press. *Dark Salt* is the first volume of the trilogy. *Orphan Stars* and *The Lesson Longest Learned* will be the other volumes. Hugh Fox, eminent critic and dean of American poets, has called Strongin the most exciting poet writing in America today.

www.ingramcontent.com/pod-product-compliance
Lightning Source LLC
Chambersburg PA
CBHW052210090526
44584CB00016BA/1998